The Character
of Christ

# The Character
# of Christ

*Harold A. Bosley*

Abingdon Press
Nashville
New York

THE CHARACTER OF CHRIST

Copyright © 1967 by Abingdon Press

Library of Congress Catalog Card Number: 67-22163

Scripture quotations unless otherwise noted are from the Revised Standard Version of the Bible, copyrighted 1946 and 1952 by the Division of Christian Education, National Council of Churches and are used by permission.

The text of the poem "In Christ There Is No East or West" by John Oxenham on p. 114 is used by permission of Miss T. Oxenham.

The text of the hymn "We've a Story to Tell to the Nations" ("A Message to the Nations") by H. E. Nichol on pp. 137-38 is copyright and is used by permission of H. E. Nichol, Kirkella, Hull, England.

The poem on pp. 81-82 is from Fred Eastman, Men of Power, Abingdon Press.

SET UP, PRINTED, AND BOUND BY THE
PARTHENON PRESS, AT NASHVILLE,
TENNESSEE, UNITED STATES OF AMERICA

To
The Faithful Congregation
of
Christ Church Methodist
New York City

# Contents

# Introduction

Over one hundred years ago, in 1858, to be exact, Horace Bushnell published his epochal work, *Nature and the Supernatural*. While trained theologians were immediately and deeply interested in the entire book, one section of it excited widespread interest in this country and abroad among laymen as well as clergymen. It bore the special heading, "The Character of Jesus," and the illuminating subtitle, "Forbidding his possible classification with men." So popular was this section that it was printed separately and has made its mark as one of the classics in modern Christian theology. Bushnell was one of the pioneers in the breakaway from the rigid, if

9

not arid, dogmatic structures in which the Christian faith found itself entombed at the beginning of the nineteenth century.

The point that interests me just now is the fact that Bushnell found in the character of Jesus—in his life as lived and reported in the Gospels—the firm foundation for Christian faith.

Now, a century or more later in our radically different world, on all levels of life and thought we hear those theologians who proclaim that "God is dead" taking their final stand on *the centrality of Jesus Christ in faith*. Whereas Bushnell was set to the task of finding evidence for God in Jesus Christ, our God-is-dead thinkers have the infinitely more difficult task of trying to find evidence for meaning in life in Jesus Christ without benefit of God! Of course, they are attempting the impossible. Take the meaning of God out of the life and teachings of Jesus Christ, and there is no meaning at all. He was what he was, and he is what he is because of his relationship with God.

Regardless of the side we take in this contemporary theological debate, the ancient and significant fact remains that when men see Jesus Christ, they see in him the true meaning, structure, and purpose of life itself— whether called by the historic name, "God," or not.

The unqualified and uncontested importance of Jesus Christ in man's understanding of himself and history is the point at which this series of homiletical interpretations began. It is intended as a companion volume to

*The Mind of Christ* and centers attention on some of the moral and ethical qualities in the life and teachings of Jesus Christ that have disturbed and comforted men for nearly two thousand years.

The field of New Testament scholarship is a lively arena these days, and widely varying estimates of the historical value of the gospel narratives cause one to move among them with caution. Yet, finally, they must be used because they are all we have and because each Christian must come to terms with Jesus Christ and say what he finds in him. For we talk of him as a present fact, not as a museum piece in history. We find him to be a firm and decisive companion, one who seeks certain goals and demands a genuine moral discipline of his disciples. He made it perfectly clear that it is not enough for men to praise him; he seeks loyal and obedient followers.

I find it disturbing that many churchmen today shrink from and sometimes appear to belittle the very notion of "following Jesus." While this can be hopelessly superficial, it need not be so. The ones "who upset the world" were following Jesus. They asked their listeners to join them on that journey no matter where it led. The first name given to the disciples according to the book of Acts was "followers of the Way." Only men of action can become centers of action in this world. In a time of moral confusion only those who aspire to and try to achieve a high level of moral direction and discipline can hope to lead in the search for a creative kind of moral stability. To this end, the Christian community is dedicated.

I hope the succeeding pages will make it clear that this reexamination of certain qualities in the life of our Lord is no explicit or implicit call for a retreat to the moral code of the New Testament; rather, it is an attempt to explore and appropriate the moral qualities exalted there in our search for a decent human family today. We are engaging in what can only be described as a strictly contemporary and wholly existential venture!

## Chapter 1

# MEEKNESS

SCRIPTURE: Matthew 5:1-14

TEXT: "Blessed are the meek, for they shall inherit the earth."

### I

I would not for the world call Mr. Norman Cousins, famed editor of *Saturday Review*, a catfish without defining my terms. But since I do want to call him just that, let me define the word.

In the old days when the fishermen out of Gloucester, Massachusetts, tried to bring back their fish alive, they had to fight the tendency of the codfish to settle down in the bottom of the huge tanks and stay there with little or no activity. When this happened, they either died, or their flesh lost its tang. Someone discovered that a catfish in the tank would keep the cod all stirred up—and in best of health.

Mr. Cousins serves churchmen as the catfish served the cod; he keeps us all stirred up and, hopefully, in good health.

I am referring specifically to his poignant editorial in a recent issue of *Saturday Review*. Writing of the "tragic flaw" in our efforts for peace, he says that new and fresh impulses for peace must come from "some" source if the United Nations, or any other organization, is to be of much help. He points to the "total subjectivity" in our point of view, whether personally or nationally, and calls it the "tragic flaw" in all our efforts for peace. Actually, we have no ideas of how to end war as a form of human behavior. All we have been able to do is to change policy or strategy or seek some end politically. Mr. Cousins goes on to the observation, "It is difficult to say where the new realizations and energies will come from." With that he lets the matter rest. But I cannot let it rest, for, to me, it is a probing judgment on the actual existence and integrity of the nine hundred million persons living today who call themselves Christians! Can it be that we have so far fallen from the insights of our faith that we have nothing to say that might be a saving word?

The stinging challenge of this question underscores

the urgency of renewed effort on the part of the Christian church to inquire into the answer we are trying to make to the moral disturbances of our day. But the answer must be incarnate; words alone will not do.

As an introduction and possible outline to the answer implicit in our faith, let us center our thought on various aspects of Christian character as we see them in the life and teachings of Jesus Christ. The one with which we begin is "meekness"—for which there is but one text: "Blessed are the meek, for they shall inherit the earth."

To those who ask, "Why begin with Jesus Christ?" I must say that unless we Christians begin with him, we have no point of beginning, no point of departure, no direction to take, and no place to go—as Christians. If you ask, "Why begin with meekness?" the answer is a little more difficult. It would have been more acceptable, I suppose, to begin with some manlier virtue— courage, determination, sacrifice—but none of these goes more directly to the fundamental need of our time than does the virtue of meekness.

I grant you it is an almost hopeless task to get a hearing for "meekness" at a time when we are tooling up our emotions for the hatred, the self-righteousness, the self-pity, the arrogance of war. Nevertheless, the issues at stake are too grave for us to pay much attention to the odds against our getting a hearing for the things that must be said. We must count on the possibility that, in the providence of God, a still small voice may yet be heard above the hurricane of our time. If so, let that still small voice be one of Christian conscience raised in search of its own nature and purpose.

## II

Admittedly, meekness has always had a bad press. It has been misunderstood and misrepresented by friend and foe alike. Properly understood, however, it is an essential Christian virtue and a courageous and manly one as well. As we study it, we shall find it a badly needed virtue in our behavior today.

We are familiar with the many misrepresentations of meekness. It has come to be synonymous with weak compliance, a listless acceptance of anything and everything, a sort of doormat philosophy of life, a point of view that appears to make us glad to be walked on by someone, just anyone.

Leo Durocher, eminent baseball player and manager, is noted for his rough talk and rough ways. Some years ago during a hot race for the pennant, he was asked to give his opinion of Mel Ott, then manager of another ball club. Durocher replied, "Mel is a nice guy, but nice guys finish last in this league."

Each time I try to visualize the misrepresentation of meekness, I think of Durocher's words and paraphrase them to read, "Meek guys finish last in this league." If that is true, why would anyone think the meek would inherit the earth, rather than be ground into it under the ones who take advantage of them?

No question about it, though, meekness is a sort of prodigal son among Christian virtues. It has taken a journey into a far country and wasted its original substance in careless interpretations. It is high time for it to return to its original meanings because it is fundamental, not alone to Old and New Testament thought, but to any successful understanding of the Christian ethic and life.

The Greek word for meek, πραος, is interesting. It is used to describe wild horses that have been tamed and trained; it means wild horses which have been gentled to the point that they are able to work with men. The selection of that particular word by early Christians is provocative and prophetic. Meekness means channelled and directed energy. The meek are those whose explosive, driving vitality has been channelled and directed by conscious and loving obedience to God as found in Jesus Christ. The meek are the spiritually trained folk, and the trained person will triumph over the untrained one every time. Small wonder an early Christian writer refers to the "work of meeking," meaning the continual training of the Christian in hearing and obeying the will of God through love.

## III

The basic understanding of meekness can be summed up this way: It has been called "attendant disposition, born of humility, which enables the soul to bow without complaining before the will of God in the hard and perplexing experiences of life."

Meekness, then, shows itself—defines itself, if you will—in three closely related attitudes: toward God, toward others, and toward one's self. Let us look at each of these, briefly, as we seek a clearer and firmer understanding of it.

Meekness begins, continues, and ends before God. It is basically an attitude which grows out of a consciousness of God and our relationship with him and with other people before him. The meek person is humbly submissive, alert, and obedient in the presence of God, and faithful to the leadings and promptings of God. He accepts, quickly and quietly, the disciplines of faith and life suggested to him by his relationship with God. He never for a moment confuses himself with God, but is deeply and keenly conscious of his creaturehood under God. Therefore, he faces the unfolding of God's will in the "hidden issues of the future" with the calm and trustful faith that it will be for his good, even though it should lead him to a Gethsemane and a Calvary. Without full faith in the reality of God and in his will and purpose for life, we see that meekness not only is no virtue, but it has no meaning at all, for it begins and ends before and in him. It is a way of listening to God and being willing to obey him. It is a way of loving God and trying to serve him through obedience and trust.

18

Meekness relates man to man as well as man to God. The meek person seeks to live in a truly distinctive way in his relationships with other people. He accepts all people as children of God, and he hopes to be accepted by them in the same way. Therefore, he reaches out toward all in a spirit of compassion and understanding. He builds bridges, not barriers, between and among men. He does not build walls that separate; he opens doors and windows enabling people to see and communicate with each other. He does this with the clear understanding and realization that upon occasion he will be imposed upon by harsh, self-seeking, arrogant men. Even so, he does not reply to them in kind or treat them as they treat him. He learns to control his natural impulse to retaliate in anger, and there is only one place to learn this—in the presence of God himself. Thus, through love and forbearance, he remains master of himself in every situation, for God's sake. In the presence of injustice and provocation, meekness is the capacity to restrain one's self through love of God.

We ought to be warned by the fact that meekness is not always an innocent virtue. It can be quite provocative in its own right! Do you remember Aesop's fable in which the wolf insisted that the lamb's meekness was most provocative? Even so, meekness does not mean we lose the capacity for indignation in the presence of evil, but it does mean we will make that capacity serve reason, firmness, and justice. We will never "explode" in the presence of injustice. We will know we can serve

God, not by inconstant, fitful, if not blinding gusts of emotion and passion, but by a constant fidelity to his will for the good of all who are involved in the situation.

It is hard to overemphasize the difference meekness makes in human relations. The meek man will view all men with the kind and quality of compassion which helps him understand and appreciate them, and he will do this because he is grateful to God for whatever God has given him. He believes God has both given him life and made him a trustee and steward of it. Therefore, his life is supposed to be lived by an ever-deepening involvement in the lives of other people. A hard, self-centered person goes through life blind and calloused to the true spirits of everyone he meets. He never really sees anyone but himself. He never really feels the bite of any need but his own. He is guilty of what Mr. Cousins calls the "tragic flaw" in life: total subjectivity. He is guilty of what Ralph B. Perry once called the besetting sin of our generation, our "egocentric predicament."

The meek person must be eternally on his guard against this sort of thing—not only in others, but especially in himself. He knows every man is burdened to the point of breaking by a load that is all he can possibly carry, and he does not want to add to that load. He realizes every human being needs the help of friends, comrades, and kindred spirits. Understanding this, he literally reaches out toward others, especially those in dire need of creative fellowship. As he reaches out, however, he does so in the name and for the sake of the God in whom he believes.

The meek person has a very simple understanding of himself; he is not his own—he is a child of God; he is God's man, if you please. He believes this to be the deepest truth about himself as well as other men. While this assurance will not spare him adversity, loss, and all manner of hardship common to man, it will give him the courage and strength he needs to triumph over them. His body, as Paul said, he will treat as a temple of God. His relationships, to follow Paul's reasoning, he will treat as given to him by God and precious in the sight of God. He sees his life as an instrument through which God's will may be worked in the affairs of men. Never for a moment will he say, as some moderns do, that life is a chance creation in an alien cosmos or that each one of us is entombed in a cell of aloneness from which he cannot escape, or that the history of man is as meaningless as the pulsations of the ceaseless waves against the eternal shores.

As we believe in meekness, we will have an entirely different estimate of ourselves, others, and our common destiny. Meekness is no cloistered virtue. It is an invitation to a kind of quiet heroism in life. One may flinch from its demands but will never refuse the hardest tasks and will walk the most impossible paths indicated by God's will. For he knows that "with God, all things are possible."

Considerations like these make it a little easier to

21

understand what our Lord had in mind when he said, "Blessed are the meek, for they shall inherit the earth." To translate this into our own vocabulary, "Blessed are those who have accepted the discipline of love and obedience to God; for they alone have the will and the strength to inherit the earth."

## IV

But meekness is not a word or even a careful definition; it is a way of life—and if we are going to understand its true meaning, we must get acquainted with some of the men who are presented to us as being meek, for meekness is as meekness does.

In the book of Numbers we hear Moses described as being "very meek, more than all men that were on the face of the earth." That, I suppose, is the source of the answer we were supposed to give in my Sunday school days to the question, "Who was Moses?" We were to answer, "Moses was the meekest man who ever lived." When I think of Moses as a meek man, however, I realize I am not only standing in the presence of a strong man, but of a strong virtue as well.

I think of his call to leave the peace of home and oasis and to return to the tensions and turmoil of Egypt. The call came from the "burning bush." He was curious enough to approach the bush but terror-stricken at what he heard, for the voice of God called him to return to Egypt to set his people free. To say that

22

Moses shrank from the undertaking is to put it mildly. He demurred, he begged, he expostulated, he argued that he was not the man for so tremendous a task. Four different times he tried to escape it. "Who am I that I should go to Pharaoh, and bring the sons of Israel out of Egypt?" he wanted to know. When the voice insisted, Moses cried, "But they will not believe me!" Still the insistent voice said, "Go." Moses pled, "Oh, my Lord, I am not eloquent. I am slow of speech and of tongue." Still the command to go to Egypt. "Oh, my Lord, send, I pray, some other person."

But God was insistent, and Moses went. He stood before the Pharaoh time after time until he had permission to take the children of Israel out of Egypt. Then he led them across the Red Sea and into the barren wastes of the wilderness. He went to Mt. Sinai. There he received the law, brought it back, and gave it to his people as the heart of their life—the very soul of Israel. He led them in the wilderness. He held them together when their new-found freedom seemed to weaken and fail. He kept them on their course even when they wanted to turn back—ready, like Esau, to trade their birthright of freedom for a mess of the good Egyptian pottage of security. He led them to the edge of the promised land and then turned them over to Joshua, confident that God had raised up a new leader of his beloved people.

What did this meek man get done? He found a people in slavery and left them free men. He found a people engulfed in superstition of all sorts and led them to a new faith in one God. He found them separated from each other and knit them into an unbreakable unity through the law. He left the mighty stamp of one of history's greatest figures on their life and law and on ours as well.

When Numbers tells us that "Moses was very meek, more than all men that were on the face of the earth," it is saying, in effect, "He was a selfless servant of God. He was humble before God. Once he had accepted the mantle of responsibility, he did not try to take it off. It was his, given to him by God, and worn as a trust before God."

V

In the Christian tradition we think of Jesus Christ preeminently when we think of meekness incarnate in human life.

Jesus was born in humble circumstances. He spent all but the last few years of his life as a carpenter in Nazareth in Galilee. At thirty years of age he was called of God into the public ministry and, like Moses, drew back from it. The story of the temptations in the wilderness suggests all too eloquently his turmoil of mind and soul, but he accepted the call and took to the highways and villages of Palestine with the good news of the gospel—the news that God's kingdom had come and was open to all. He had many listeners, but won few disciples. He accumulated many critics, but found few supporters. He went wherever people were and showed the very heart of God's love in his dealings with them. Even when it was clear that the high hopes of his disciples for the imminent coming of the kingdom in clouds of glory were not to be realized, he persisted in his mission to the bitter end. He was the victim of as vicious a frame-up as ever took the life of an innocent man. His critics got him and put him to death. He died alone, so far as friends were concerned, having only two thieves as companions. Yet, through it all, he was conscious of God, of the love of God, and of the need to obey him. How else shall we understand that tragic, yet triumphant, prayer, "Not my will, but thine be done"?

But death could not hold him. His disciples, scattered by fear, were reunited by faith and sent to the ends of the earth.

What did this meek man achieve? No one would be presumptuous enough to try to sum it all up, but it is clear that he is the pivot on which our history turns. He taught us that God is love; that love is the law of life; that the kingdom of God is the kingdom of love; that that kingdom is open to all men; that all who love God and neighbor utterly may enter it, and, as they do, they will become new persons.

When he said, "Blessed are the meek, for they shall inherit the earth," he was talking about men who have received a special gift from God through a vital relationship with him. They are humble before him always. They seek, above all else, his will and the strength to do it. And God will provide that! Empowered and guided by him, they will be the ones who can actually make the effort to live as he wills on the face of this earth. Only one who is willing to obey him can hope to do that! God is central; obedience to God is fundamental; and there is a willingness to serve him through adversity or prosperity. These are the weapons with which the "terrible meek" face life and the conquest of this earth. Meekness has truly been described as a "world-conquering principle." It does not conquer by returning evil for evil, but by overcoming evil with good —positive, virile, affirmative good.

## VI

I think it is high time we put a great sign outside of every church—a man-wanted sign which reads: "Wanted: More meek men." We desperately need men who, in return for their life, will embrace the entire world—men who are humble enough to pray, sensitive enough to learn, cooperative enough to try, in the face of every failure, to bring men together across every chasm that now separates them from each other. We need men who are firm enough to face the great issues of life unflinchingly and to do so in the name of God. We need meek men, men of God, and we must have them if ever we are going to make an effective proclamation of the

Christian gospel in the church and, through the church, to the world in which we live.

We need a generation of men who are trained in spirit, as well as in mind, if we are to keep those who are trained in mind and skills alone from destroying the earth. We are finding it much easier to put a man on the moon than to swallow our pride in the pursuit of peace. We would rather run the risk of blanketing the earth with a cloud of deadly fallout and destroy the whole human enterprise than admit we have been head-strong, arrogant, and mistaken in foreign policy. Any way we want to look at it, science has placed in our hands the tools that now threaten to make a mockery of every fair dream we have ever had for the life of man on the face of the earth. The weapons of war—the refined product of our most disciplined research—are now pretty largely in the hands, or at least at the mercy, of moral morons. The more intelligent we are, the more insane and brutal are our actions. The more disciplined and devoted we are to the knowledge we have, the more we spread chaos and anarchy throughout the world until and unless we can find some way of breaking out of this vicious circle.

Meekness points the way; it is the one thing needful if we are to make a new beginning. Dr. Bentley Glass, distinguished scientist and biochemist, has recently called attention to the relationship between values and science, and he makes, in his own way, the point I am trying to make—namely, that science left to itself will

27

ruin the world. Its unparalleled capacity to enrich life will be subordinated to its incredible efficiency in the destruction of life unless it can be made to serve values that come from the field of religious faith. That is where meekness comes in—as a kind of spiritual discipline learned in the presence of God himself. Only as a life is disciplined by the adoration of God, faith in God, love for God, and a desire to serve God, will it be disciplined to the point where it can speak a word of direction, with power, to the scientifically trained generation of which we are a part. We cannot separate ourselves from the "bundle of life," from the family of man. We are in it far more deeply than we can ever know. It comes down to this, doesn't it? If we will not learn to love one another, we do not, therefore, escape kinship with others; we merely transfer our mutual relationships to the arena of self-destruction. We either love our neighbor, or we hate him; these are the only alternatives offered us in today's world.

When I think of meek men of today, I think of the late Albert Schweitzer. It is not necessary to sketch his life or sing his praises. Many people have either met him or have come across his name so many times that they feel at least a speaking acquaintance with him.

Dr. Schweitzer surely lived at the opposite extreme from the kind of life most of us seek. His quietness contrasted with our loudness; his purpose with our aimlessness; his serenity with our anxiety; his hope with our despair; his peace with our tension.

We could ill afford to lose him from our life today. He was a kind of living conscience for us all. He was a meek man, one whose obedience to the quiet insistent will of God led him to strange paths of service and peace. He pointed a way—a far from perfect way, to be sure—but a way in which we may proceed as we seek to develop better relations across the face of the earth.

My favorite picture of him is one taken on a forest path, alone, at the close of a busy day. Though his aging body is stooped with weariness, there are lines of peace on his face.

When I think of meek men, I think of Martin Niemoeller, too. He is one of the "terrible meek" of whom Charles Kennedy wrote. Terrible—not because they threaten to destroy us—but because they threaten to destroy the false images we have created of ourselves and our work. No one will say Dr. Niemoeller lacks courage or vision or purpose in life.

To know Martin Niemoeller is to trust and love him because he trusts and loves people. He was on a trip to Viet Nam with some of us in the summer of 1965, and we had a chance to become acquainted with him all over again. He was a member of a small group that went by bus on a long and dangerous trip deep into the Mekong Delta. While the rest of us looked out of the windows with some apprehension at the ominous, yet lovely, countryside, Dr. Niemoeller slept like a baby. He did not even rouse up when we passed through one group of armed guards after another on either side of every bridge we crossed. He was not only a meek man; he was a man at peace with whatever might happen.

With humble childlike faith in God and his love, Martin Niemoeller has helped us believe that those who counsel despair are wrong, that there is work, gloriously hard and tragic, to be done by all who are willing to live for God's sake and in his name.

Yet, whenever Dr. Niemoeller spoke to us of his faith, my mind went through several flashbacks, and I asked myself, "Is this quiet, sincere little man the one who had the courage to answer an outraged Hitler's demand that the churches leave the German people to him with the firm word, "They are our people, given to us by God."

In another flashback I saw him in the concentration camp for years—never once surrendering to despair but ministering in Christ's name to his fellow prisoners, always confident that even that experience would work for good under the guidance of God.

Still another meek person who has meant much to me is Jane Addams—noted social worker and leader of the human spirit of a preceding generation. One of the luminous memories of my days at the University of Chicago was the convocation service where she received an honorary degree and made a speech a short time before she died. When she died, an atmosphere of unbelief settled over the entire city of Chicago. The poor people of the city, whose voice she had been for more than a generation, lined the streets on which the funeral procession was to pass.

She had been more than their spokesman; she had been their voice—not in an exalted sense, perhaps, but in a down-to-earth sense of meeting their need. One day in the City Hall she was getting into the elevator very early in the morning. The elevator man, knowing her very well, said, "What is it this morning, Miss Jane, garbage cans or incinerators?" Smiling, she answered, "It's garbage cans today."

Jane Addams had the capacity of relating garbage cans to the kingdom of God in such fashion that common people knew the meaning of her concern for them and their daily welfare. In her lifetime she more nearly represented the poor people of Chicago than any and all of the political leaders put together. That is why they stood in awe, if not in actual apprehension, of what she might say and do. She was a little person, physically, but within her small body were a powerful mind and a radiant spirit that enabled her to stand up to the representatives of the power structure of the city. Quietly, firmly, conscientiously, this meek person spoke in behalf of the things that represented a better life for every person in the city of Chicago, and particualrly for the poor people.

Such persons, I submit, will inherit the earth if any human being does. Only they have a chance to do so, and only they deserve to do so. The rest of us, left to ourselves, may kill each other off like wild beasts in the jungle. We will try to kill off the meek, too, because they will be opposing the things we stand for. On the face of it, it should be easy to dispose of them. In a sense it is, if we deal with them one by one. We can kill them but then our troubles are just beginning; they don't seem to stay dead. Their lives, being lost in God, live forevermore in and through him and continue to lead men to respect and obey him and other human beings as his children. They and they alone will inherit the earth—and this by the will of God.

## Chapter 2

# HONESTY

SCRIPTURE: Luke 8:4-15
TEXT: "And as for that in the good soil, they are those who, hearing the word, hold it fast in an honest and good heart, and bring forth fruit with patience."

## I

In studying the character of Christ we are centering attention on certain values or qualities in his life which have come to be regarded as essential in Christian ethics and Christian character. We must be ready to do more than discuss them; we must incarnate them, and that calls for spiritual discipline of the highest order. Only the disciplined life can make an impression for good in the troubled world in which we live. The moral disorder that has overtaken us moves at too deep a level for surface objections and surface protests to be effective. The Christian ethic, rooted as it is in the profound insights of the Christian faith, goes to the depths of human life and speaks to the human situation today. It is there in the depths that we are discovering anew the meaning of the virtues that made the character of Jesus Christ the powerful fact it is in human history.

When we lift up honesty as an essential virtue, we must do so with the full recognition that all religions do likewise. Honesty is prized wherever men think seriously about life. That is why it is one of the essential virtues in Christian ethics. It is not too much to say that there can be no Christian character, witness, or society without a firm emphasis on the basic value of honesty, truthfulness, and integrity.

Most of us, I think, recognize the fundamental need for honesty and sense the fact that it is a kind of moral cement that holds society together. A stable society of liars is unthinkable. Emerson said, "Every violation of truth is a stab at the health of human society." Even our jokes about lying have a very serious point. Recall, if you will, Mark Twain's advice, "When in doubt, tell the truth." He practiced what he preached, too! When writing his book *The Private History of a Campaign That Failed*, he began by warning, "I am an experienced, industrious, ambitious, and often quite picturesque liar." George Bernard Shaw jolts us with his word,

"My way of joking is to tell the truth. It's the funniest joke in the world."

Not so in our religious heritage. Christianity has never regarded honesty as a joke. The will and the ability to know and to tell the truth are serious matters. Neither can we agree with Ben Franklin's maxim that "honesty is the best policy" for the simple reason that we do not think of honesty as a policy at all. Honesty is a quality of life or character rather than an adopted procedure of behavior. Honesty has to do with the structure of conscience, will, and heart—not with a deliberately designed and carefully weighed kind of social behavior. Honesty is not a policy we can adopt; it is a set of soul we must win. That, at least, is the clear biblical and classical understanding of it.

## II

Jesus' familiar parable of the soils relates honesty to the heart. You will recall that the same seed fell on different soils with radically different results. When Jesus was interpreting the parable to the disciples, he said, "And as for that in the good soil, they are those who, hearing the word, hold it fast in an honest and good heart, and bring forth fruit with patience."

The heart, then, is a soil in which the seed falls, and obviously there are various kinds of hearts: hard, stony, thorny, shallow, as well as "honest and good." This suggests that any understanding of honesty must begin with a quick look at what biblical writers think of the "heart," the seat, the abode, the source of honesty. The notions of what the heart is and does are part and parcel of the biblical understanding of the component parts of our essential nature.

The heart is one of three basic elements in human nature; the other two are the flesh and the spirit.

The *flesh* is the seat of all carnal, earthy desires, appetites, and passions—and as such is the source of evil impulse and desire. Nevertheless, the flesh is never wholly or necessarily evil; it can be good, too, as when the Psalmist cries, "My flesh faints for thee." Basically the flesh is of the dust. It is composed of what God took from the ground in the day of creation. It is the part of man most unlike God, for into it God breathed his spirit that man might become a living soul.

The *spirit* is the quality of divinity in man, the Godlike part of his being which was breathed into him by God in creation. The spirit is the seat of wisdom, strength of will, firmness of faith, and obedience. By spirit man is able to commune with God—as like communes with like.

The *heart*, the third point in the triangle of the human being, is vitally related to and can be deeply influenced by both flesh and spirit. It corresponds to our idea of soul or self in which both the divine and earthy elements are found. The heart, then, is the central, the controlling instrument of decision and life, for both flesh and spirit must exert their influences in and through the heart of man. It is a battleground where the two meet and have it out in their struggle for the control of life. What the rabbis came to call good and evil impulses ride into the heart like white and black knights to joust for the control of thought, word, desire, and deed.

The heart is described in many ways, but always as the hidden, invisible, inward member of the basic qualities of life. It is the deepest level of personality, for in it the true life of the person is fashioned. In and through it man lives as man—not as God. It is the seat of conscience, moral choice, and conduct. It is the organ of understanding and knowledge. When David had had his orgy of sin, it was his heart that "smote him" and brought him to his knees before God.

To say a man has "no heart" is to say he is without understanding. To "steal one's heart" is not a romantic theft at all; it is to deceive one's understanding and betray him into evil. The deep springs of one's life well up from the mysteries of the heart. As long as the heart is good, that is, is guided by reason, understanding, and intelligence, its issues in life are good. When it is under the domination of passion and evil impulse, the issues are evil.

This sort of understanding of the heart lies back of the well-known biblical words: "As he thinketh in his heart, so is he." (Proverbs 23:7 KJV.) "Keep thy heart

37

with all diligence; for out of it are the issues of life."
(Proverbs 4:23 KJV.)

The Psalmist in search of a vital relationship with
God prayed, "Search me, O God, and know my heart!"
And when he asks the question, "Lord, who shall abide
in thy tabernacle? who shall dwell in thy holy hill?"
he can find but one answer: "He that walketh up-
rightly, and worketh righteousness, and speaketh the
truth in his heart." (Psalm 15:1-2 KJV.)

Jesus underscored the ancient creed of his people:
"Hear, O Israel: the Lord our God, the Lord is one;
and you shall love the Lord your God with all your
heart, and with all your soul, and with all your mind."
He taught his disciples: "The good man out of the
good treasure of his heart produces good, and the evil
man out of his evil treasury produces evil; for out of
the abundance of the heart his mouth speaks."

Although subsequent generations have witnessed
several revolutions in our understanding of man, the
Christian faith continues to regard the heart as the
symbol, not alone of man's creaturehood, but also of
the dignity and responsibility of life. Actually, this
emphasis is an overwhelming vote of confidence in
man on the part of the biblical writers. We are so
constituted by God that we can know him, can serve
him, can search for him in each generation, can know the
truth, and in it can find our freedom. But we must
be honest about it all—honest about God, our fathers,
and ourselves as we face the issues of our day.

## III

Honesty, to put it simply, is the determination to tell the truth in any and every situation. This does not mean that an honest man always tells the truth. It does mean that he always tries to tell the truth. An honest man can be mistaken, but he will be honestly mistaken. Honesty most emphatically is not a strategy; it is a set of the soul. It is the thrust for integrity on the part of a human being.

As such, it includes far more than what we say or the words we speak. It is a matter of our entire life. It is what we are as well as what we say. To say of one, "He is an honest man," is to say something about his habits of thought, the way he reaches decisions, the manner in which he understands people and problems, as well as the way he speaks. Honesty is a matter of character as well as of speech.

Honesty is the breath of life to every creative and enduring relationship we know and need. Name them over: friendship, love, marriage, home—can you imagine these being other than centers of misunderstanding and conflict if the ones who share in them do not trust the honesty of each other? There is no place for the liar, the cheat, the deceiver, the double-dealer, the two-timer in any of them. When dishonesty replaces honesty in these basic personal relationships, dissension and dissolution are inevitable.

Honesty is more than being able to account for

income and expense. It is a symbol of personal integrity. It involves one's entire being. It is a quality of character and must be "of the heart" in the biblical sense of that term.

## IV

There are four steps we must take if we would learn the discipline of honesty as we find it in the character of Christ: (1) We must love the truth; (2) we must seek the truth; (3) we must be obedient to the truth; (4) we must speak the truth *in love*.

Easier said than done—of course it is! But the attempt must be made by any and all who admire and aspire to any degree of Christian character.

*First, we must love the truth.* If the skeptic wants to ask, with Pilate, "What is truth?" he is asking a good, but quite different question and one that requires separate handling. For the moment, we accept as valid the ordinary understanding that a kind of objective order of events is a fact and that we live surrounded by such events. When someone says, "It's 93 million miles to the sun, or 25,000 miles around the earth, or that it is 15 miles from the Harlem River to the Battery, or that the national debt is 300 billion dollars, more or less," we know that all of these statements can be true, untrue, or approximately true. An honest man tries to tell the truth about life as he sees it, feels it, and knows it. He must be honestly skeptical and doubtful about interpretations that seem to him to be untrue to fact. He must love the truth, have an open and avowed passion for it, be obsessed by a determination to pursue it, and, if at all possible, try to lay hands on it.

Theoretically, at least, the Christian should find it easy to love the truth since he believes: (1) that there is a truth to be found; (2) that it is of God; (3) that in Jesus Christ we have a full revelation of God's truth for the meaning of his will for our life and destiny. The Christian begins, then, with the basic conviction that the love of truth is the love of God or, if you prefer, that the love of God is the love of truth. Therefore, he will desire, above all else, to know and to serve this truth of God.

But the truth we love will both limit and free us. Make no mistake about the limitations; they are real. As we love the truth, we will hate evil with a holy passion. Our love for truth will deny us easy rationalizations of evil thoughts, evil habits, and evil plans. It will deny us the kind of moral and ethical compromises that actually cheapen us, even though they seem to ease the pathway at the moment. Only as we accept the limitations can we know the fullness of the freedom that truth alone can bring. The freedom to know, to accept problems as real, to entertain and be fair with questions and doubts, to share with others in the search for better understanding of common problems—these are the daily fruits of freedom. We are freed by the truth to give tongue to our deepest doubts, fears, and hopes, which,

41

in a sense, is the finest fruit of freedom known to faith.

The honest man, as he loves the truth, will seek it—seek to find God's will, way, and purpose for his life, relationships, and times. We are not given much more than a glimmering of the truth at any time—this we know. The ones who seem to find it work, sacrifice, and suffer in their search for it. Charles Kettering, himself a great inventor, once said of the research scientist, "He must not bruise easily." The same may be said of the truthseeker in all realms.

We feel the rigor of this commitment when we probe many of the questions before us at the present time: What is the truth of the claim that the Civil Rights movement has passed the peak of its power and influence so far as this country is concerned? What is the truth of the charge that the church is the last stronghold of conservatism in our society? What is the truth of the claim that we not so much share in the United Nations as use it as a tool of our foreign policy? What is the truth of the assertion that the present administration's policy on Southeastern Asia is a dangerous and bankrupt adventure in "old-line colonialism" in a new garb?

Or, to raise a slightly different set of questions: What is the truth of the statement that while more people are joining the church, fewer people are going to church? What is the truth of the claim that religion has a larger influence in the life of this country than any other country in Christendom?

If anyone steps up and says he has an easy answer to

questions like these, we know him to be an imposter. There are no easy answers lying anywhere this side of a careful, disciplined critical search for facts. Even when all of the relevant facts are assembled, there may be honest differences of opinion as to the proper interpretation of them. Each time I am tempted to leap into quick judgments on such matters, I recall something Plato wrote, "Seven years of silent inquiry are needful for a man to learn the truth, but fourteen, in order to learn how to make it known to his fellow man."

An honest man will have to forgo the gleam and glitter of sweeping generalizations and flip answers and be content to move along the roadway of fact step-by-step. And if he cannot find enough to warrant a conclusion, he must say so—and continue the search.

But if and as he finds the truth, or thinks he finds it, the honest man will be obedient to it. The truth is not so much his tool, as he is the tool of truth. The man who would find the truth must be willing not only to learn but also to be led by what he finds. Galileo was led to the brink of heresy by what he found. Luther was led out of the Roman Catholic Church by what he found. The Pilgrims were led to this fair land by what they found in their determination to worship God according to the dictates of their own conscience.

Some time ago I heard two brilliant research scientists talking about their work. One asked the other, "Where is your research taking you?" Taking you! I like that! It lays bare the kind of obedience to fact that is required of an honest man.

A few years ago the name of a wonderful young evangelist was on the lips of religious leaders in this country. He was a very successful preacher—especially with young people. He worked in the Presbyterian Church and with the National Council of Churches. As a matter of fact, he spoke at a meeting of the Evanston Council of Churches the year before he suddenly dropped out of the picture. The deepest reason for his action came by way of one of his friends, "He wasn't as sure as he thought he ought to be about some of the things he had been saying. He wanted time to think them over." Who can help honoring a man like that? I do not regard it as a defeat for him or for the church. Rather, it is the simple testimony of an honest man that his loyalty to truth had led him in directions he had not anticipated and could not explain to himself or to anyone else without further investigation.

Obedience to the truth never leads by still waters alone. It leads one through storms of doubt, uncertainty, criticism, and sometimes into open collision with the status quo and the powers that be.

Listen closely to the heart of our heritage, and we will hear men crying, "We must obey God rather than men!" "God helping me I can do no other." We will see men like Bishop Francis J. McConnell facing the wrath of the steel industry in Pittsburgh in the '20's as he determined to discover for himself, the church, and the conscience of this country, the truth about the living conditions and wages of the steel workers. We will see Dr. Willis Tate, President of Southern Methodist University, facing the aroused critics of his school, denying their charge that he coddles communism and refusing categorically their request that he let them step in and run the school. And we will see the students of that university holding a great and spontaneous mass meeting to express their appreciation of his obedience to the truth. An honest man must be obedient to the truth no matter where it leads him.

An honest man, nurturing Christian character, will love, seek, and obey the truth, and he will speak it in love. That, I am sure, is the distinctive thing about the Christian witness to truth, and it is the hardest requirement of all. How to stifle our indignation over the evil he does sufficiently to speak the truth in love to the evildoer is almost beyond the grasp of mortal man. There are not nearly enough instances of it in Christian history to reassure us as to its possibility. Actually, we see the vials of bitterness filled to overflowing and dumped on one another's head with appalling frequency by our Christian forbears. Yet, unless we can learn to speak the truth in love, we will speak it in bitterness and hatred, and these inevitably will cancel out the healing effect of whatever truth we seek to speak. When we speak the truth in bitterness or hatred to anyone, we not only close his mind to what we say, but we confess our unworthiness to say very much at

45

all to him, for bitterness and hatred are major sins and are as destructive of Christian character as any evil which may arouse them.

Every parent knows that he must learn how to speak the truth in love to his children if he is to be much help to them. Without it he will lose their confidence immediately. Every teacher of any consequence learns the same hard lesson. No amount of brilliance and wit can compensate for a lack of personal concern and understanding in a teacher. A teacher who cannot clothe the truth in honest concern is a poor teacher, no matter how right he may be in what he has to say.

Only as we seek to be honest, as we try to love, seek, obey, and speak the truth in love throughout the whole range of life, can we claim to nourish a Christian character within ourselves, our children, our life and time.

V

How I wish it were not so hard to be honest in the things that really matter! It is ever so much easier to shade the truth, to evade it, to refuse to tell it either to ourselves about ourselves, or to ourselves about the situation in which we may find ourselves.

Yet, we need to be honest with ourselves about ourselves. This, of course, recalls the role of the confessional in the historic church. When I say confessional, I am not meaning necessarily the wooden box type of confessional which we see in many churches, but rather the honest pouring out of one's soul to a sympathetic ear. Some of us cannot do this easily; perhaps some of us cannot do it at all. In any event when we do it, we do so at great cost and in great confidence. But it needs to be done in the interests of the normal health of a person—especially a person who has lost confidence in himself. Only by being honest with oneself about oneself can the deep sense of guilt be lifted and can we enter a new day when our energies are released from the burden of guilt and we are free to face the issues that lie ahead of us.

Some years ago a free-lance journalist, George Seldes, wrote the book *Tell the Truth and Run*. It deals with several public figures and events about which journalists, who knew the truth, were either afraid or were not permitted to tell it at the time it occurred. So Seldes, waiting until he was almost dead himself, published his version of many of these events.

One thing is clear: It may be possible for a journalist to tell the truth and run, but faith cannot do that; *faith must tell the truth and stand*—stand by it, stand for it, and stand to the bitter end. Our Lord told the truth about the Temple, the Pharisees, and the leaders of his people—and he stood his ground when they closed in on him to put an end to his life. Before Pilate and the high priests he might have sought a prudential formula that would have enabled him to save his life, but he stood his ground, even when death was the only alternative to some kind of compromise.

We expect and honor integrity in the scientist. We expect him to tell the truth and stand by it. We expect him to tell us what he discovers in the laboratory and in other studies. We honor as light-bearers men like Copernicus, Harvey, and others whose fiercest battles were with colleagues in science who refused to face the new facts on which these men were basing new theories. We were properly shocked, some decades ago, when Stalin tried to settle a controversy among Soviet biologists by invoking the party line! Who would ever think that chromosomes behave according to party lines!

Yet, are we equally faithful to the right and the duties of honesty in other reaches of our life? How honest is thought about democracy and democratic procedures, for example? One of the great things about democracy is the high premium it places on honesty. Every citizen has the opportunity, the right, and the duty to be informed, to be concerned, and to be honest about the issues before his country at any given time.

We are presently undergoing a retesting of this right to be honest. When we challenge the wisdom of our foreign policy in Viet Nam, we find our patriotism impugned; we are told that we give aid and comfort to the enemy. Whether it is Senator Fulbright and his distinguished committee or the General Board of the National Council of Churches speaking up critically about this new and utterly dangerous war, the ancient effort to curb honest criticism and dissent rises from an increasing number of sources.

If we cannot or will not be openly and outspokenly honest in critical times over grave issues, are we not, in effect, saying that honesty is a luxury to be enjoyed only in quiet times and on unimportant matters? In other words, is *conformity* rather than *honesty* to be the guiding virtue of democracy? Yet we know that this cannot be true. If it were true, then democracy, as we have understood it, is a delusion—and I for one do not believe that for a single moment. I believe in democracy most passionately, and because I do believe in it, I am certain we must tell the truth as we see it, openly, freely, and forcefully until we are either proved wrong, or the truth prevails. We must tell the truth and stand fast, or what we say we are fighting for in South Viet Nam will be a mockery here at home.

In similar fashion honesty is a vital value and is at stake wherever the issue of academic freedom is being raised. We see it raised now in many places—in tussles between state legislatures and state schools, as well as between church authorities and church schools. The easy answer, and the one usually made, is to say that if a professor believes something that is shocking to the body politic or to the church authorities, he ought either to be fired or forced to resign. Yet these answers contradict the basic meaning of honesty. If the question the critic is concerned about is an honest one, it ought to be given an honest answer—and firing him is a dishonest answer. An honest question must be answered where it is raised—within the community of scholars of which

49

the questioner is a member. Both he and the question, whether it questions the validity of democracy as a political theory or belief in God as a theological doctrine, should be taken in hand and dealt with openly, honestly, and firmly by his colleagues and by no one else!

The tragedy and the glory of Jesus Christ lie in his determination to be honest, to seek and to tell the truth about God, about himself, and about other men and their relationships with each other. He was honest; he tried to keep things in a divine perspective. He was honest in his dealings with the scribes and the Pharisees. He was honest in his dealings with critics and friends alike. Where it was most difficult to be honest, namely, with his family, he continued to say what he thought ought to be said even though his family drew back from him for a while.

To me one of the crowning examples of his honesty came when upon one occasion he and his disciples were in the Temple observing the ones who came and went in the Holy Place. They saw a poor woman, a widow, come in furtively, drop two small coins in an offering box, and then leave quietly. Soon thereafter the great givers, accompanied by trumpets, came with their big gifts. People probably gathered around and congratulated them upon their generosity and looked forward to the many good things that could be done in the Temple with such fine gifts. Jesus looked at all this with clear and honest gaze. He said to his disciples,

"The poor woman has given more than all of the others put together. What she gives comes from the depths of her need. Her two pennies have hurt her worse than the large gifts have hurt the ones who have given them. Because she has given from her very need, her gift will mean more to the Temple than any other." This is being realistic with a vengeance, don't you think? Yet, can any of us deny the justice of what he said? Do we not need to keep ourselves and our gifts in some such perspective as this? If we do, we shall proceed with a great deal more honesty when we think in terms of what we are giving to the church. We shall ask whether we are giving until it hurts; whether we are giving from our need, rather than from the margins of our convenience. That is the honesty of our Lord brought to bear upon our behavior in the church today.

If there is tragedy—and there will be—and if there is glory—and there may be—in the service of Jesus Christ, then it will lie in the determination of persons like ourselves to live as he lived on this matter: to be honest, to seek, and to tell the truth about ourselves, about our relationships with each other, and about our God and our relationships with him as we see him in Jesus Christ.

Seeking, as we do, to achieve a more abundant life for all men and a kingdom of love in the affairs of men, we must be guided, in all honesty, by loyalty to the truth and follow it faithfully all the days of our lives. Our comfort and our strength will be this: In the service of truth, we find the meaning of freedom.

## Chapter 3

## PURITY

SCRIPTURE: Mark 12:28-34
TEXT: Jesus answered, "The first is, 'Hear, O Israel: The Lord our God, the Lord is one; and you shall love the Lord your God with all your heart, and with all your soul, and with all your mind, and with all your strength.' The second is this, 'You shall love your neighbor as yourself.' There is no other commandment greater than these."

I

Some years ago, Dr. Philip Jacobs of the University of Pennsylvania was asked by the Hazen Foundation to carry out a comprehensive study of *Changing Values in College.* He and his colleagues discovered, among other things, something they labeled the "undercutting of moral values" in college life. They found this in the gradual acceptance of cheating on the part of many students, also in the growing toleration of other forms of moral laxity.

We have felt the truth of this in the cheating scandals that have swept across many major campuses in this country. We have been very close to it in some of the high schools and colleges situated in and around the metropolitan area of New York City. We know that the educators are not talking about an abstraction when they talk about the "undercutting of moral values."

Actually, this phrase suggests one of the reasons why we are living in the vortex of a moral revolution. It would be serious enough if this upheaval were confined to the younger generation and particularly to the college campuses, but we know that its effects are much wider. We see the undercutting of moral values in business and professional life, in personal and social relationships, and in private and public dealings. We have seen instance after instance of public officials betraying the trust of their office and being driven out of those offices, facing disgrace and often serving prison sentences. Small wonder popular journals are now concerning themselves with discussions of moral disintegration and speculating on the nature of a new morality which may be emerging.

Yet, when we stop to think abut the pounding we have been taking over the last hundred years, the marvel is that any historic moral values at all have survived. Moral values do not exist in a vacuum; they are an integral part of life. They belong to and draw their life and meaning from many things, principally, religious faith and social institutions such as family, community, and the social order in general. When these supporting factors are relatively stable, moral values are certain to be firm and generally accepted.

During the last hundred years we have seen all such natural allies of moral values battered almost beyond recognition and their hold on life badly shaken. It began with Darwin's *Origin of Species* and ended with *The Kinsey Reports*—with the intervening years being one red continuum of wars, revolutions, and climactic social and technological upheavals that affected the structure of society much as the great earthquake of 1906 affected San Francisco.

## II

However much we might wish it otherwise, the simple fact is that we must do our thinking about the meaning of Christian character in an atmosphere of decidedly confused moral thinking. That is why and where Christian values such as purity come into sharp focus and widespread misunderstanding.

I must confess that I hesitate even mentioning the word "purity." For some time it has usually meant to superficial critics of Christianity something like the three little monkeys who see no evil, hear no evil, speak no evil. Yet any sustained search for the moral values in our religious heritage requires that we look at the concept of purity, and when we do this realistically, our little monkeys disappear forthwith!

Like other great values, purity is hard to catch in the net of a single definition. It means so many different things when found in different settings. We see this in a vivid way in the biblical interpretations of it.

In the Old Testament we discover purity in four related but quite different settings: ritual purity, racial purity, moral purity, and spiritual purity.

Ritual purity means that the law had been kept, the proper sin offerings brought to the temple, and the rite of cleansing performed. The earlier books in the Bible, particularly Leviticus, Numbers, and Deuteronomy, are filled with detailed instructions on how both to avoid sin and be cleansed of it in order to be able to approach God in his holy temple.

Racial purity became an obsession with the Jews following the disastrous experience of losing their freedom and their nation and going into exile as captives and slaves. Resolved that it should never happen again through sin on their part, the remnant who trekked back for a new try determined to separate themselves

55

from the contamination of others by walls, laws, customs, and a severe ban on intermarriage with Gentiles. The books of Ezra and Nehemiah are more than records of courageous and sacrificial actions; they are hard chronicles of the curses and punishments inflicted on all who sinned by marrying outside of Israel. The books of Ruth and Jonah are vivid protests against the excesses to which the drive for racial purity actually went in the life of Israel. The long genealogical records in the Bible were thrown up by this grim determination to have or, at least, to claim racial purity.

Moral purity was associated almost exclusively with sexual relations. It meant the acceptance of chastity as binding always upon women and usually upon men. The Hebrews, offended by the sex orgies of the nature cults that flourished around them, deepened their original suspicions of the evil nature of sex. Anything relating to sex was suspected of being the carrier of evil and sin and was to be guarded with ceremonial fidelity at all costs.

Spiritual purity not only encompassed other kinds of purity, but added the dimension of complete, sensitive faith in God. The prayer of the Psalmist, "Create in me a clean heart, O God, and put a new and right spirit within me," points up the meaning of spiritual purity. It suggests a life lost in God—a life of obedient faith in God's covenant, promises, and providence. The longest psalm in the Psalter—the 119th—is a sustained eulogy of the need to love and follow the law of God if one is to be pure before him.

Against this background of history incarnate in living law and institution, it is not hard to see how and why purity was a fetish among many devout Jews in Jesus' day. A careful reading of the Dead Sea Scrolls introduces us to a little sect that was determined to be pure in the sight of God, no matter what it cost.

The New Testament gives the Pharisees a rough time of it, but, to be fair with them, we must begin with a simple observation: They were devout folk—determined to keep themselves pure before God by living their entire life according to his law. We must not let the excesses to which they surely went blind us to the driving moral and spiritual purpose in their effort. As so often happens, though, they became preoccupied with the things they should not do, lest they sin. Purity quickly became a negative virtue or, rather, a matter of negations rather than affirmations. Morality increasingly became a list of "Thou shalt nots" rather than "Thou shalts." It became preoccupied with increasingly fine points in externals: food, clothing, and observable behavior. It is one of the sad axioms of human nature that when we begin to measure the worth of a morality by such externals alone, it becomes an affair of externals through and through.

According to New Testament records, this is what Jesus believed was happening to the lofty moral codes of his fathers. Though as interested as the most devout

Pharisee in the total meaning of purity before God, he was shaken into open and sharp criticism of the externalism of prevailing religious morality. As Leslie Stevens wrote, "He [Jesus] rediscovered the inner pole of morality." He insisted that a clean cup required scouring on the inside as well as on the outside. He made it plain that purity begins, continues, and never ceases being an affair of the heart. It will and it must control behavior and lead to humility before God and a sincere desire to help man. We ought never to forget Jesus' summary of the law that was designed to keep Israel holy before God: "You shall love the Lord your God with all your heart, and with all your soul, and with all your mind, and with all your strength . . . [and] your neighbor as yourself."

This is his formula—if we may call it that—for purity. It is a life made radiant by a genuine, all-consuming, all-embracing love for God and man. From this sort of love, deeds of penitence before God and helpfulness to man inevitably come.

In several other ways Jesus described the meaning of life purified by a sincere love of God. He likened it to the innocence of little children who are capable of loving someone simply, completely, and happily and whose complete trust is given with their love. One who loves God this way will be blessed with singleness of vision. That is the meaning of the Beatitude: "Blessed are the pure in heart, for they shall see God." Or, as Shafto has interpreted it, "The secret of happiness in life is with [the] single-hearted; they shall see God in everything."

This emphasis on purity is the most distinctive part of the Beatitudes. There are antecedents to almost all other Beatitudes in previous Rabbinical teachings, but nothing really precedes this. It was struck up and out of Jesus' own thought and experience. Purity, as he uses the word, means (1) being free from lust and evil desire; (2) having a single-minded loyalty to God; (3) being completely obedient to God's will. The word "heart" in the Beatitude means not the organ that receives and expels the blood in the circulatory system, but the whole person, the real center of our being.

Every housewife will appreciate the fact that one of the meanings of "pure" in the New Testament is "clean" and "white" and is used in connection with a freshly washed garment. Our Lord is saying that those whose minds and spirit have been cleansed of sin are able to see God. For the phrase "see God" means not to behold him with the physical eye, but to know him in spirit and in truth, to see him in daily life—in the lilies of the field, and in the birds of the air—to hear him in the laughter of little children.

But this capacity to see God in everything is reserved for those who love God with all their heart, soul, mind, strength, and their neighbor as themselves. This kind of love results in purity of motive, purity of thought, purity of mind, and purity of life. Thus, our Lord is saying that the pure soul will neither commit adultery nor want to do so. It will neither kill nor hate. All such evil desires and impulses will be expelled by the power of the all-pervasive love for God.

This, then, suggests the reality of both the inner and outer poles in the moral teachings of our Lord.

One of the most profound tributes to him and his teachings on purity is wrung from the reluctant pen of Nicolai Hartmann, a German philosopher, who believed it possible to construct a system of ethics without reference to God or religious faith. But when he came to a discussion of the value of purity, he admitted he was dealing with a very great yet essential mystery. He writes in *Ethics*,

Purity of heart is a primal Christian virtue. . . . With this estimate Christian ethics opened up new roads. . . . Purity is the basis of a series of well-known moral values: sincerity, frankness, openness. . . . One who is pure has nothing to conceal . . . . He does not need to mislead others. . . . He believes in the good in man . . . . He trusts in the right and the good cause . . . . He is optimistic in a child-like way. . . . He cannot comprehend the gnawing ethical pessimism which imputes evil to everyone. . . . Nothing works so powerfully, so convincingly for good, and so transforms others in their inmost character as the mere presence of a pure-minded person . . . . This power is the secret of purity . . . . The great example is in the figure of Jesus . . . . At the sight of Jesus, by His mere word, shrewd calculation and subtility are silenced. Here, certainly, the spiritual superiority of the person supplements the idea itself; but, behind it is something else which gives support to it—the moral pre-eminence of purity of heart . . . . Perfect purity borders on holiness.

## III

"Blessed are the pure in heart, for they shall see God!" This summary of blessedness lifts up the drive for inner cleanness, for purity, for holiness as an essential part of the nature of all confessing Christians, and it has blazed up with hope each time the Christian faith touches a person. Men have gone to incredible lengths in their quest for purity. The mystic, the monk, and the seer are alike in their appreciation of it and desire to win it. Francis of Assisi renouncing worldly ways and wealth; Ignatius Loyola turning his back on one life and hewing out another; John Bunyan tirelessly obedient to the inner light; John Wesley's incredible half century of religious leadership—these are a few examples of men in quest of purity akin to holiness.

Am I not right in this: There is a hunger in each of us for a simpler, more direct, more honest kind of life than we usually live? We are sick unto death of all the complexes, inhibitions, repressions, and frustrations that tie us in knots. We cheapen ourselves in everything we do and everyone we touch with the laxity of our loyalty, the hypocrisy of our ways, and the double tongue with which we speak. We understand Fitzgerald's agent who cried, "I find myself falling on my knees in wayside shrines, praying that I shall not end by being tawdry."

The adult delinquents among us may chuckle upon occasion at the salacious jokes, the smutty shows, the double-talking comedians, who seem to delight in smearing precious things, as well as the horde of writers whose productions profane every sacred thing in the name of *realism*—which, in translation, means a story so sexed-up that Hollywood may be interested in buying it. For such persons, purity is a joke. What they do comes under the heading, "In Praise of Vulgarity."

But not for men like Will Rogers. How glad I am Oklahoma selected him as one of her representatives in the Hall of Fame! In the summer of 1965, Eddie Cantor wrote a wonderful reminiscence of him in the *Today Magazine*. I am thinking now of the incident which, Cantor claims, caused Will Rogers to drop out of the play *Ah, Wilderness* shortly before his death. Rogers had received a letter from a minister who told of taking his teen-age daughter to see the play. He did so, confident that Rogers would never appear in a role of questionable character. He was so shocked and embarrassed by what he saw that he and his daughter got up and left before the play was over. He wrote this to Rogers, and, says Cantor, the letter so upset Rogers that he soon asked to be relieved of his part in the show.

Without presuming to comment on the entire episode, I want to pay tribute to a man like Will Rogers on this as well as on many other accounts. Purity would not be an offensive virtue to him, for it would mean integrity, sincerity, and uprightness.

Actually, in any serious thought about Christian character, purity—purity of motive, mind, thought, and life—must be placed on a par with honesty, mercy, meekness, and firmness. Our mind is more than a squirrel cage in which we pursue one measly little thought after another; it is the organ whereby we may think God's thoughts after him. Our will is not simply a power for bending others to our service; it is the power to curb self-interest in the service of God. Our body need not be, or seem to become, a crawling jungle of undisciplined desire and appetite; it can be a temple of God.

Chastity in thought and life is an honest Christian alternative to unchastity. Fidelity in marital relationships is the Christian alternative to infidelity. Honest and honorable dealings in business and professional life are the Christian alternatives to dealings of other sorts. From the point of view of the Christian faith, it is more than silly to weaken our lives by intemperate habits; it is a sin against the love and the intention of God in granting us the gift of life itself.

Smut, fashionable as well as vulgar, is one of the tempting and besetting sins of our time: smut on newsstands, smut in books, smut in shows, smut in conversation, and elsewhere. Smut is a dirty, reprehensible cheapening of sacred things. And if it should seem necessary for us to besmirch ourselves with it in order to live in this world as some claim, then it is high time we change the character of this world.

It may sound like trying to turn the clock back to pre-Freudian days to say it, but the Christian emphasis on the sacredness of life calls for purity, not prudery, for singleness of vision, not confusion of purposes, for a persistent desire to let our life be lost in God, not in the service of ourselves. In doing this we are not so much trying to unlearn whatever truths Freud may have taught, as to remember the infinitely greater truths taught by Jesus Christ.

And when we study, with open mind and listening spirit, this essential in Jesus' own life as well as in his teachings for his followers, we discover a full-orbed emphasis on things not to do as well as things that ought to be done. Purity does lead us into a consideration of what one does not do, does not say, does not think, does not propose. It also leads us to the much higher plain of determining what we ought to do and what our ideals ought to be if we are to serve the kingdom of God. Purity causes us to concern ourselves with the great duties of life—duties that grow out of the love and the service of God as well as the love and the service of man.

## IV

We live in a day of low visibility and foggy visions, morally speaking. What is it that fogs up our moral windshields and keeps us from seeing clearly the road we are trying to travel? Hate, fear, anger, selfishness, pride—these are what obstruct and distort the visions of all of us these days. While it is true that 20-20 spiritual vision is unusual in any human being, most of us need some help if we are going to see with any degree of clarity and accuracy the way to go in our dealings with other people. The hateful man can see many things, but nothing as it really is. What he sees is in a nightmarish setting rather than the white, clear light of God's will. I know it is an open question whether or not we can ever see anyone clearly or hope to see him as he appears to God, but that need not keep us from trying to see him with as much clarity as possible. If we begin with the simple assumption that he is a child of God, beloved of God, dear to God, then there rests upon us an unlimited responsibility to react to him in that light. Faith in God and faith in man manifested in our love will clean the windows of our soul, and all of us need to have those windows thoroughly washed. If we are so blinded by hate that we cannot see another person or a people clearly, how much less can we hope to see God? When we think of the ways in which we are blinded by the simple mention of the words "Russian" or "communism" or "China" these days, we get some notion of how easily we are blinded by our own fears and hates.

Bad as it is to have a distorted view of man, it is

worse to realize that unless we can see man clearly, we cannot hope to see God. Actually, the matter works both ways. Unless we see man, we cannot see God; unless we can see God, we cannot see man in his truest sense. Therein lies the genius of faith. It enables us to place ourselves completely in the keeping of God by an act of trust and to learn, however unworthily, how to think his thoughts after him. We may be sure that under his tutelage we shall not learn to hate and distrust one another. Rather, we shall learn the meaning of loving our neighbor as ourselves.

But the God whom we love and seek to know better is a moral being. That is, he insists that we make the effort to see other men as he sees them. And he is serving an ultimatum upon us in our time, one that we see in the crescendo of hate and distrust. Out of this holocaust comes the fateful warning: "Learn to see other people truly, or die in your blindness."

Purity is not an optional aspect of life; it is an essential attribute of a strong purpose in life. It is an essential quality in the life of mankind if men are to continue on the face of this earth. But the way to this kind of purity begins precisely where Jesus said it did: with a centering of life in the love of God and man. Gamaliel Bradford was right when he cried, "Without God, everything crumbles." That is surely true of purity. Without God it is not only unattainable; it is unthinkable. But with God and through a sincere love for him and loyalty to him, our lives can be blessed by singleness of purpose, openness of outreach, and a continuing thrust toward complete integrity. Once more we will become what we very much want to be—whole beings, persons made whole by the love of God in our lives.

*Chapter 4*

MERCY

SCRIPTURE: Luke 23:26-38
TEXT: "Father, forgive them; for they know not what they do."

I

We are surely bucking the current of contemporary life when we present mercy as an essential value. We live in the age of the "tough guy"—an age in which hardness, not mercy, is exalted as a great virtue. We live at a time and among a people who glory in the "body count" of the enemy and call it a victory when the count rises high in the numerical scale. Ours is not an age in which compassion is praised in our dealings with one another.

In fact, we tend to regard mercy as being synonymous with sentimental pity, and we think it a form of weakness. Does it seem to you as it does to me that increasingly the hardness, which is an item of faith in the code of the juvenile gangs that have been terrorizing certain sections of our large cities, is becoming a characteristic of the day in which we live? If so, ought it not be a matter of great concern to all of us?

Some of us will recall a telecast of recent date showing the completion of a new air base in the northern portion of South Viet Nam. The commander was being interviewed and was asked how he felt about having the base ready. He said, "I'll be glad to get the fighters in here. Then we can get at your job of killing Viet Congs. I'm anxious to kill a lot of 'em!" He said it in a very matter-of-fact way, and as I heard him, I was chilled, not alone because he was speaking for himself but also because he was speaking for so many of us.

There is little mystery about the way hardness has become a virtue for us. It has been a long time reaching its present status, at least four hundred years. It began with the Renaissance—that period in Western history when man began to find new confidence in himself and to lose his old consciousness of God. When that happened, humility began to dim, too. Man transferred his adoration from God to himself; pride ceased to be a vice, as the medieval fathers had regarded it, and became a virtue. With the elevation of pride came self-confidence, assertiveness, and a consistent playing down of mercy and compassion. While these were not wholly forgotten, they were regarded as soft sentiments rather than strong virtues. They were thought to be good qualities for women dealing with children, but not for "practical" statesmen dealing with other nations and other people.

Nietzsche caught the true meaning of this trend. Indeed, he became its most perfect embodiment in his famed gospel of the superman. He asserted that mankind stood on the threshold of a great new epoch of creative achievement if only the fetters of old ideas, values, and relationships could be broken by supermen. Under the guidance of such spectacular and occasional spirits, a higher culture and a prouder race blessed by audacity, firmness, and a will to power would emerge. The strongest impulse in man, argued this dark genius, is the will to power. All men have it, but few are capable of letting it come to full expression. And to those few belong the honor and tragedy of breaking the bonds of all that inhibits man and of surging forward to a new manifestation of power. The will to power leads to the will to master not only one's self but as many others as possible. All the brutality of trampling down those who may be in the way, all the unfettering of the primitive beast in human nature appear here as the right and duty to be strong. The strong man unfolds and defends the energies of living against a morality for slaves which emphasizes humility, meekness, and mercy.

The way of Nietzsche is the way taken by modern

man: power, more power, still more power—power through science, power through technologies, power over nature, power over others. Except for the faint pipings of conscience heard in occasional lulls, mankind's frantic lunge for power has gone unchallenged save by the awful consequences that have begun to take fórm in depressions, revolutions, wars, and now the specter of the annihilation of life from the face of this earth.

It goes without argument that the experience of being nurtured in this culture has conditioned most of us to idolize power, the hard man, the ruthless victor, who is capable of sweeping all before him.

Our religious heritage believes in strength and in strong men, too, but it incorporates mercy and compassion among the essential virtues of our understanding of strength. "Why mercy?" you may ask, and the reply must be, "Because it is an essential attribute of God"— as Shakespeare expressed it so powerfully in the immortal soliloquy on mercy which comes from the lips of Portia.

## II

Though there are many men and moments in the Bible that seem to be totally devoid of anything that resembles mercy, we discover it exalted repeatedly as one of the essential ways of knowing and serving God. Psalm 136 is a brilliant illustration of an ancient emphasis on mercy. There are twenty-six verses in this psalm, and the concluding refrain in each one is "For his mercy endureth for ever" (KJV). Twenty-six different ways in which the Lord has favored Israel are chanted by the priest as he faces the people in the Temple; twenty-six times they reply, "For his mercy endureth for ever." A different translation of this phrase renders it, "For his steadfast love endures for ever" (RSV). In biblical thought mercy grows out of the steadfast love of God. Because God loves man, he is merciful toward him. Mercy, then, represents the hand of God's love reaching down to men at the point of their deepest need for him.

But the mercy of God is more than his hand reaching toward man; man's mercy toward other men is really the mercy of God manifesting itself through human hands. This is Micah's thought as he summed up our religious duties in his immortal question: "What does the Lord require of you but to do justice, and to love kindness, and to walk humbly with your God?"

When Jesus was on the cross, he lifted the prayer perfect of the merciful soul. Thinking of those who were putting him to death, he said, "Father, forgive them; for they know not what they do." From that moment intercession in behalf of enemies has been an essential expression of Christian character. When Stephen was falling under the stones of Paul's mob, he cried, "Lord, do not hold this sin against them." Until we learn how to pray for those who hate, curse, and despitefully use us, we have not scaled the summit of the Christian expectation of our life. It takes the strongest kind of Christian even to attempt it, as well we know if ever we have made the effort. The acid test of faith lies precisely at this point: Can we sincerely pray for the welfare of our enemies? It requires so much of us that most of us will not even attempt it, and we may even want to know why we should. But before we give it up, let us see what we are losing when we lose mercy—or what we are gaining if we achieve it.

## III

*Mercy is of God.* It is the steadfast love of God for all men. When we say God is merciful, we are saying that his love is tireless, endless, always seeking man out, no matter where or how he has strayed from or rebelled against God. God's mercy means more than that he wishes us well; it means that he is actively seeking our welfare. Mercy, so conceived, is a practice, not a sentiment—a fact which Jesus never tired of stressing. For him, mercy is to be one of the required attributes of any man who enters the kingdom of God. Even as men are saved by the steadfast love of God, so they must be the channels through which that love flows steadily into the lives of others. Only one who extends mercy to others can actually receive it from God. Mercy, then, is more than the note of kindness in the Christian temper; *it is the act of reaching out in compassion and under-*

73

*standing to anyone*—no matter what he has done. It is a way of forgiving one over and above any desserts he may have. It is done for God's sake, as well as for our own and for the sake of others.

Our fathers used to make much of the phrase the "mercies of God" in their songs and prayers. It is much too precious a phrase to lose, as even a quick look at it will prove. They made a helpful distinction between two kinds of mercies—daily and special. Both are in evidence in the Bible and in our own experiences. As a matter of fact, they are so much in evidence that we tend to take them for granted. It is a salutary thing to remind ourselves of the down-to-earth, human quality of them.

The daily mercies of God are most easily taken for granted and understandably so. Food, shelter, friends, loved ones, work, play, the beauties of nature, the warmth of affection, the joy of little children—these are the building blocks of daily life. Usually, we do not even think about them until we miss them. We are like the little fellow who got around to thanking his Uncle Herbert for a Christmas gift along about March 25. He did it with this note: "I'm sorry I didn't thank you for my Christmas present, and it would serve me right if you forgot about my birthday next Thursday."

The seasons come and go, bringing with them seed-time and harvest. The warm sun, the life-giving rain and snow, the good earth and fertile seeds, and the teeming seas—all conspire to make possible the food we eat, the clothing we wear, the houses we live in, even the kind of air that is favorable to life unless we so pollute it that we are poisoned by it. Yet, we easily fall into the habit of taking all of this for granted. Edward Everett Hale once said there was enough religion in a grain of corn to drive an atheist to his knees. He was thinking of the wondrous cycle of events by which the grain could fructify, grow, and nourish life. Once we see the mystery and sense the meaning of it all, we will believe in God and thank him, or so Hale thought.

Many of us do not react that way, though. Our response is more likely to be that of a certain five-year-old boy whose mother had spent an unusually trying spring day taking care of him and his two younger brothers: dressing, washing, and feeding, from 6:00 A.M. to 6:00 P.M. Overtaken by a headache, she had gone to bed, and the father, trying to keep the children quiet, said, "Let's keep quiet. Mother is resting; she is awfully tired." The oldest boy stopped what he was doing and asked in honest amazement, "Why is she tired? What did she do?" He had taken it all for granted—like the sunshine, the air, and all else that made up his usual day.

This is understandable in a small child (I'm sure no mother would hold it against him), but it is regrettable when a mature man walks that blindly among the daily mercies of God. We are all guilty of it much of the time, and it is not hard to see why. We are chained to the clock, the calendar, and the schedule. Our responsibilities seize us by the throat with the first glimmer of consciousness in the morning and shake the life out of us the livelong day and sometimes far into the night. Under these circumstances it is hard to be properly sensitive to the deeper meanings of the daily mercies of God. It is easy to fall into the habit of taking them for granted.

But when we stand in the sanctuary, surrounded by the timeless, the unhurried, the eternal beauty of his holiness, we share the Psalmist's experience. "We have thought of thy lovingkindness, O God, in the midst of thy temple." As we do this, we may well be moved to share in a prayer such as this:

O thou most holy and ever-loving God, we thank thee once more for the quiet rest of the night that has gone by, for the new promise that has come with this fresh morning, and for the hope of this day. While we have slept, the world in which we live has swept on, and we have rested under the shadow of thy love. May we trust thee this day for all the needs of body, soul, and the spirit.

## IV

Strangely enough, we get into the habit of taking the special mercies, as well as the daily ones, for granted. Whereas our fathers would say of some special blessing, "God has been good to me," we are inclined to say, "I was lucky," or "It was just my day." It is more serious than first meets the eye to switch our loyalty

76

from the providence of God to the wheel of luck; yet, many of us have done just that.

Crises come the way of all, and it is in connection with them that we experience the special mercies of God most keenly. It is no accident that primitive religions have two kinds of religious ceremonials: the *periodic* ones that occur regularly and the *special* ones that occur when a great need arises. When Columbus set foot on the New World, his first act was to kneel in gratitude to God for his special mercies on the long hazardous voyage. When the Pilgrims were safely on shore, they too thanked God for his care. Neither would have understood any other reaction. When wars begin, our sanctuaries are filled with heartsick people needing and seeking the guidance of God through the holocaust. When wars end, men seek the sanctuaries again to thank God for the end of killing and to pray for his guidance in preventing its ever happening again. Even though some will forget the sanctuary soon after, theirs is a sound instinct. We ought not take the special mercies of God—his willingness to steady, to strengthen, to guide us in adversity—for granted. We ought to do everything in our power to keep keenly alert to them, lest we ask of God, "Why? What has he been doing?"

Sickness, whether in ourselves or in a loved one, presents a special spiritual challenge to all concerned. The management of sickness calls for spiritual resources of a high order. Sickness imposes a new regime on life.

It changes the routines by which we live and breaks up the regular patterns of existence. As such, it lays an unusual assessment on our physical, mental, and spiritual energies. Some of us, by the mercies of God, have the reserves to pay the bill; others do not and are spiritually bankrupted by it.

Take, for example, a sensitive middle-aged woman, who is coming to the end of the long and difficult vigil of caring for her invalid and now dying father. Years have passed since she has stood in the sanctuary meditating on the loving-kindness of God. She has been too busy for this. Now, cracking under the strain, she says, "I think I am quietly going mad." She isn't, obviously, but she is in trouble, serious trouble, because she has been so blind to the daily mercies of God that it has never occurred to her that there are special mercies of patience and steadiness sufficient for the challenge of sickness.

Contrast her situation with another like it. The same challenge was there, but this time it was met by one who had learned how to "go with God" through each of her days. I do not say it had become habitual, but I do say it had become a regular part of her daily life. Consequently, she faced her challenge, not thinking she was going mad, but confident that God would see her and her loved ones through. And he did. When it was over, she said, "I have never felt that we were alone in this." Will you not agree with me she received the special mercy of trust and the patience that came with it?

78

We do not live long without discovering that the best-laid plans of men and mice often go astray. Changes, not of our own choosing sometimes, are forced upon us. Few problems put our spirits to a more severe test than to find ourselves doing what we had not planned to do, or not doing what we had planned to do.

If the matter is important enough, fear and anxiety knock at the door and, if admitted, bring despair and panic into our souls. But, thanks be to God, there are other callers seeking admission: faith and trust in the providence of God. If we let them in, they will bring the spiritual strength we need to work steadily, patiently, and hopefully at the changes which confront us. The ancient advice "Trust in the Lord! Be not afraid!" is excellent modern therapy. Whether ancient or modern, it must be ranked high among the special mercies of God that no man can afford to take for granted. The poet was right:

> I steadier step when I recall
> That, if I slip, thou dost not fall.

The refrain of one of our best-loved hymns puts the sentiment in words we have sung from our childhood:

> Where he leads me I will follow . . .
> I'll go with him, with him all the way.

The practice of standing in the sanctuary and thanking God for his loving-kindness will serve us well when the days of special testing come. We will then turn to him as naturally as a flower turns toward the light, and we will do so confident that we are never alone in our difficulties, that somehow his will is somewhere in the problem, and that we will find the right answer only as we find his will and are guided by it.

## V

Jesus said: "Blessed are the merciful, for they shall obtain mercy," or, as it may be translated, "Blessed are the compassionate; for they shall receive compassion."

How could it be otherwise, if God is a God of love? If his every effort to reach us is born of love and seeks an expression of love in and through us, how can we help thinking of him as a God of mercy or of ourselves as men of mercy?

"Ay, there's the rub!" We are ashamed to talk of mercy because it is in such violent contrast to the way we live, and we are honestly shocked at the thought that we ought to become men of mercy. Yet, I cannot think of mercy without thinking of deeds of mercy and lives of mercy.

During my first year at the Divinity School at the University of Chicago I heard Graham Taylor address the student body. Before I saw him, I knew him to be one of the great teachers of Christian social ethics in the life of the modern church and the father of the Chicago Commons. He had come to be a patron saint to those of us who believed that religion ought to be deeply involved in life. Years later, after he died, I understood these words one of his students, Nels Francis Nordstrom, wrote of him with the heading: "Graham Taylor —Man of Mercy":

We knew him as a child of the earth,
But that divine connection which links the clay of the
Earth with the light that illumines the sun and the
Stars made bright his life and the path he followed.
He knew the ways of men,
    The hungers, the tragedy, the yearnings of the human.
He knew the brutal realities of conflict and competition. . . .
He knew the full meaning of poverty and injustice.
    He knew the tragedy of broken lives and disillusioned
        hopes and dreams.
    He knew the ways of the city. . . .
    He knew the ways of the machine. . . .
    He lived in the shadow of hardship. . . .
He knew also the ways of the divine. . . .
Though he bore the sufferings of men,
    He linked it with the sufferings of God.
Though he bore the defeat of the human,
    He linked it with the victory of the spirit. . . .
He walked the ways of man and the ways of God.
We knew him as a child of the earth,
    But the celestial light of his soul is still
    With us as we follow

81

The man-ward path of his life, and the God-ward
    Reach of his spirit.

When I think of mercy, it is always incarnate. It is
the good Samaritan taking care of the wounded man. It
is the father running down the road to welcome home
the prodigal son. It is Jesus calling Zacchaeus out of
the tree and transforming his life by the gift of love and
confidence. It is Jesus scaling the highest peak known
to the human spirit and from its promontory saying,
"Father, forgive them; for they know not what they do."

That is the contrast. That is the choice we face in
these difficult days when the war drums get louder and
the cost of war gets heavier to bear for us and for all
men. We must make our choice as to what kind of men
we will be—or wish to become. Will we be like the taxi
driver who told me in the course of a short journey
that we ought to bomb every city in North Viet Nam
and China? "That would show them who is Number
One!" he cried.

I could not argue with him. I sat there numb with
despair at the challenge which his attitude presents to
those of us who have heard and cannot forget "Father,
forgive them; for they know not what they do." Between
these two attitudes there yawns the widest moral chasm
known to man. Yet, we must stand on one side or the
other. We either become men of mercy and proclaim the
supremacy of Jesus Christ, or we become men of hardness and follow Nietzsche. The way things seem to be

going now, the large majority of us have made up our minds: Neitzsche is lord; Christ is the deceiver! Nietzsche wins; Christ loses! Get out the cross once more and put the weak men of the world on it. That is where merciful men belong. Let the supermen of the world put them there!

But we don't honestly believe that, do we? We can't! We know it's wrong. All history stands to bear witness to the evil in that line of thinking. It contradicts everything our faith stands for, and our salvation begins with our awareness of this contradiction and our repudiation of Nietzsche and everything he stands for. Once we are aware of it and of our duty, then by the special mercies of God we may be able to climb, at however great cost, up that promontory and say each in his own feeble, faltering way, "Father, forgive them; for they know not what they do."

Like the children of Israel in search of the promised land, we are in search of a promised land today. Like the Pilgrims of old, we are in search of a new spiritual home. Like the church universal, and participating in it, we are on pilgrimage, seeking the deeper and wider kind of fellowship among all who call themselves Christians. And in all these pilgrimages we need a keen consciousness of the merciful, steadfast love of God, both as something which comes from him and something which others feel in and through us.

*Chapter 5*

# PEACE

SCRIPTURE: Matthew 5:38-48
TEXT: "Blessed are the peacemakers, for they shall be called sons of God."

## I

Finally—though perhaps too late to affect the outcome—men are universally and profoundly concerned with the problems of war and peace. What was once the localized concern of a few idealists has now become the overpowering concern of thoughtful men everywhere—idealists and realists alike. The lonely conferences on world peace held in The Hague at the turn of the century and subsequent ones sponsored by the Carnegie Foundation for World Peace have now become a literal multitude of conferences of scientists, educators, experts in finance and trade, as well as religious leaders.

Never have responsible men in the various religions of the world been more deeply concerned over any one issue than they are now concerned over peace. From one end to the other in Christendom, Judaism, Buddhism, and increasingly, Islam, this is so. The knowledge of what war is and the dread assurance of what it means have stilled sectarian strife and set us to the common task of strengthening the cause of peace by whatever means. A sense of profound urgency runs through all these deliberations.

In Christendom the two most significant documents to come out of the Roman Catholic Church of late have dealt with peace. I refer to Pope John's encyclical "Peace on Earth" and Pope Paul's moving plea before the Assembly of the United Nations in 1965. Even the Vatican Council, which was concerned with many grave issues, found itself always coming back to the cause of peace on earth.

I confess that I am unable to keep track of the many conferences on world peace now being sponsored all over the world by the member churches of the World Council of Churches. Each time I think I have a clear notion of where these conferences are to be held, I discover some others, whether in Asia, Africa, or Latin America, dealing with this same problem. In our own country the National Council of Churches has held six different conferences on the problems of world order over the last fifteen years, the latest occurring in October, 1965. The crisis in Viet Nam called into being an advisory committee on Viet Nam during the summer of 1965, and this committee has now been made a permanent part of the structure of the National Council of Churches, with the title "Advisory Committee on World Peace." It is charged with the immediate investigation of specific situations that threaten peace and empowered to recommend positions and actions to the General Board of the National Council.

Probably the most significant single development in the year of 1966 was the initial meeting of the National Interfaith Conference on World Peace in Washington, D.C. It brought together, for the first time, Roman Catholic, Jewish, Orthodox, and Protestant groups and gave them an opportunity to articulate the concerns of their faith as they bear on the problems of world peace. One of the most dramatic results of this conference was to set in motion steps looking toward a World Interfaith Conference on Peace during 1967. It is hoped that this will include representatives of all of the major religious traditions of the world—East and West alike.

The statements made and the positions adopted by such conferences do not win universal assent, of course. I know of no one who thinks they will, but I do know they are studied with great care in the halls of Congress, by the State Department, as well as by churches all across the country, if not the world. I do know that they are made the subject of intense discussion by student groups on campuses and in student retreats where, these days, there is just one burning subject—world peace. The intense and alert concern for peace, as articulated by such conferences, gives the lie to the judgments we occasionally hear that no one pays any attention to such statements. There is no evidence at all to support that kind of jaundiced thinking. In fact, whatever truth may be in it is a complete misreading of the total reorientation of religious groups toward peace. Statements adopted by conferences on peace find their way into church literature and become a part of the thought of clergymen and writers inside, as well as outside, the church. It is simply playing fast and loose with obvious fact to say that they exert no influence on the thought and decisions of our time.

Two reasons account for this universal and urgent concern of religious groups for world peace. The first, obviously, is the dire situation in which we live. Any thoughtful person knows that the life and the death of mankind hang in the balances these days. If that realization will not stir thoughtful people to action, nothing will. Thank God it has certainly stirred religious groups into a kind of action that seemed utterly impossible twenty-five years ago.

But there is a deeper reason in the Christian tradition for our concern for peace. It is our rediscovery of Jesus Christ as the Prince of Peace, as the one through whom, we believe, men will be able to achieve peace on earth and goodwill in our common life. We cannot speak of him without speaking of peace, and we cannot speak of peace without speaking of him, for the peace of which we speak is both spiritual and social in character. How could it be otherwise when we understand the age-old concern of our Hebrew Christian heritage for peace on all levels of life?

The word "peace" occurs nearly four hundred times in the Bible—more often than any other word, save the word "God." Jesus was brought up in the tradition of Micah, who expressed the deep prayer and need of mankind in these moving words:

> Come, let us go up to the mountain of the Lord,
>    to the house of the God of Jacob;
> that he may teach us his ways
>    and we may walk in his paths.
> For out of Zion shall go forth the law,
>    and the word of the Lord from Jerusalem.
> He shall judge between many peoples,
>    and shall decide for strong nations afar off;
> and they shall beat their swords into plowshares,
>    and their spears into pruning hooks;
> nation shall not lift up sword against nation,
>    neither shall they learn war any more;
> but they shall sit every man under his vine and
>       under his fig tree,
>    and none shall make them afraid;
>    for the mouth of the Lord of hosts has spoken.

For all the peoples walk
   each in the name of its god,
but we will walk in the name of the Lord our God
   for ever and ever. (Micah 4: 2-5.)

As a boy our Lord was nurtured on these words, and as a man, he made the quest for peace on all levels of life a major concern.

## II

When people heard Jesus Christ preach and teach, they heard him say, "Blessed are the peacemakers, for they shall be called sons of God." For him, peace is the divinely intended relationship between man and man, individually as well as collectively, and between man and God. Peace is an attitude of trust, of confidence, of love. Peace, as he uses the word, is not a relationship for the weak, but for the strong—for those who are strong enough to overcome injury, injustice, and indignity, and to do so for God's sake and in his name. Conflict between man and man is evil and ought to be overcome. The whole thrust of God's will and nature is against the kind of conflict that sets man over against man. The peace of which our Lord speaks is not a cheap product; it represents justice, brotherhood, freedom, and dignity in the relationship we have with each other.

At the risk of being misunderstood, let me put it

this way: God does not want peace at any price; he wants peace at his price and on his terms. This, as I understand it, is the whole thrust of the gospel. This kind of peace is possible, and whoever is willing to live with others on the plane of equality and in the spirit of fraternity will know the meaning of it. Blessed are men who live this way, for they are the ones through whom the work of God is being done on earth. "Blessed are the peacemakers, for they shall be called sons of God." Our Lord was profoundly consistent in this. The ones who listened to him heard him describe hate, fear, and injustice as the destroyers of peace within and among men. Moreover, they heard his invitation to find a new way of life in an utterly different kind of world.

What a transforming experience it must have been actually to hear him speak and reason on matters like this! When men came to him, they discovered a number of things to be true about him.

First and foremost, they found him at peace with God and with God's will for his life. He was sure of God. He felt called of God to God's work, and he had complete faith in God and in the work to which he had been called. No matter how difficult the work or rugged the way, it was his to do and his to take, and he did so with a kind of inner peace that was apparent to even his bitterest critics. He nourished his faith in God by looking at the most difficult problems in life through it and with it. He discovered something all must discover, sooner or later, that the only way to keep a faith alive is to use it and be used by it. Believing that God is love and that love is the most powerful force on earth, he determined to look at men through the eyes of love. Even when he brought their evil work under judgment as being sinful, he continued to love them and to seek for them a new relationship of trust in God. Whenever men encountered Jesus Christ, they found one in whose character peace was a central fact because love was the central power of his life.

In addition, they found one at peace with other men—with friend, critic, and enemy alike. The poise which he found in his peace enabled him neither to look down on sinners and outcasts, nor to look up to the holders of prestige, privilege, and power. One thing was needful, he thought, and one thing only: to let the light of the love of God break through the darkness of human relationships and lead men into the kingdom of God. He did not love principles; he loved persons. He did not love peace in principle; he loved the people who needed peace in order to realize God's will for their lives. Our Lord heard the crying need for God which makes all men kin and set himself to answer it in terms of concrete persons and situations.

Looking deeply into this human need, he said to Matthew, "Follow me," and Matthew, glad to give up the war he was waging within himself, against himself, and against his neighbors, answered by dropping everything and following him. Jesus looked within the tortured life and spirit of poor Mary Magdalene and invited her to a new life of purity, trust, and love. He stepped across the wide chasm between Jew and Gentile, between the Jew and the Samaritan, and spoke of the peace of God which spanned the gap and made possible the new relationship between men, and between men and God. Wherever men found him, they found one who was trying to bring into concrete existence on the face of this earth a new relationship between some person and God and the men with whom he was associated. He never spoke of the kingdom of God as though it were a principle, an ideal, an abstraction; to him it was a very present reality. It was as close as the house toward which he was walking. It could be entered as he would enter the house, by opening the door of faith and trust and stepping over the threshold. There he would find the peace of God that passed all understanding.

The ones who sought out our Lord found a man at peace with himself. How could it be otherwise in one who had found peace with God and man, as he had? He was inwardly poised and ready for the "slings and arrows of outrageous fortune," for the tricky questions of clever men, for the cruel malice of hateful men, for the honest blunderings of sincere disciples, for the shallow adoration of the crowd, who thought he was doing one thing when actually he was doing another. A man must be at peace with himself, if he is going to move with assurance through situations like these and, above all, if he is to learn to love his enemies because they, too, are the children of God.

## III

The peace which we find in him is a peace we desperately need within and among ourselves, is it not? "How," we ask, "how on this earth are people like us to find that kind of peace?"

The only proper way to conduct the search is to saturate ourselves with Jesus Christ—with his mind, spirit, life, and teachings. No man can do this for us; nor can we do it for one another. Each one must do it for himself. If we have the will to learn about him, we can do so readily enough. And as we do, certain great guiding ideas take form.

The first thing we discover as we become acquainted with the mind and character of Christ is the reality of his summary of the law: *We are to love God and man utterly.* This means, if it is to mean anything at all, that the life of faith is to be a life of love for God and man. This is what we find in him, and it is what he expects of those who follow him. This emphasis bothered good people in Jesus' day, and it has not become less bothersome with the passing of two thousand years.

The life of love is never routine; it never "stays put." It is a vital, spontaneous, creative movement. That fact was hard on good people then, and it is no easier for us today.

Jesus was surrounded by persons whose religion was no longer pliable and growing with their daily experiences. They had settled down to following certain forms from which they no longer varied and which they no longer questioned. Let it be noted, also, that they permitted no one else to question them. Recall, if you will, when Jesus and his disciples were criticized for gathering grain for food on the sabbath. That was clearly against the law of the sabbath at that time. When they were rebuked for it, Jesus answered that the sabbath was made for man, not man for the sabbath. To him, man and his needs were the really important elements in the situation—a fact which his critics had overlooked.

Jesus saw and tried to help his disciples see the hand of God throughout life—not only in world-shaking events, but also in seemingly insignificant facts like the flowers in the fields. He found and loved the presence of God throughout the whole range of creation. It will be a sad day for us if we forget, or are cease to be moved by, the tenderness with which he spoke of God's care for the sparrow, the cup of cold water, the care of little children, as examples of how to know and serve God. He never accepted the distinction between the sacred and the secular, the holy and the profane. He paid no attention to the effort of Temple authorities to limit God to the Temple. He looked at all life as of God. A flower in the field—sacred or secular? A cup of cold water to a thirsty man—sacred or secular? A falling sparrow—sacred or secular? Only one thoroughly alive to the beauty and the meaning of commonplace things could possibly have seen in them the evidences of the hand of God. But he did! And those of us who want to follow him, who want to have his mind in our mind, cannot do less.

## IV

The closer we come to him, the more we become aware of the profoundly personal nature of his belief in God and his loyalty to God as Lord of life and to the kingdom of God as the kingdom of love in life. If Jesus experienced normal doubts about the meaning of God, he had worked them out and arrived at an affirmative conclusion long before he began his preaching ministry. From the moment he stepped onto the stage of public life, every utterance radiated faith in the reality of God, in the kingdom of God, and in God's sustaining presence. His proclamation, "The kingdom of God is at hand—prepare for it!" is the clue to what he had to say to men. His invitation, "If any man would come after me, let him deny himself and take up his cross daily and follow me," is a sobering way of saying that he had hard work to do and needed helpers in it.

Yet this kingdom of God of which he spoke was not a fanciful dream created by smoking some kind of spiritual opium. The God in whom he placed his confidence was interested in a kingdom which would be characterized by the absence of bitterness, pressure, hatred, jealousy, and selfishness, and by the presence of gentleness, love, understanding, and cooperation. He was talking about a kingdom in which the great commandment would be the true guide to living.

If we let that conviction lead us today, we do not know where it may take us, but some things are very clear. It will lead us away from the pride, hatred, and fear which now cry havoc throughout the world. It will disown as evil the notion of vengeance and retaliation, whether individual or collective. It will awaken in us unqualified concern for all human need, and we will accept need as an opportunity to serve, not men alone, but God.

There can be no question that the kingdom of God, as he understood it, included and stressed the ethical concerns of life and human relationships. As a matter of fact, the nearest he ever came to losing his patience was during a discussion with the scribes and Pharisees over what things were of paramount importance in the observance of religious faith. They seemed to have great concern for the minute observance of the law and Temple rituals and precious little interest in the ordinary needs of human beings. Jesus handled them firmly: "Woe to you, scribes and Pharisees, hypocrites! for you tithe mint and dill and cummin, and have neglected the weightier matters of the law, justice and mercy and faith; these you ought to have done, without neglecting the others. You blind guides, straining out a gnat and swallowing a camel!" That's plain talk even in translation! It places the emphasis where prophetic religion has tried to keep it from that day to this—on the ethical concerns of the life of love in the kingdom of God.

Though we in churches have a hard time keeping that emphasis uppermost, I know of no other way in which we can seriously seek to be his disciples in this or any other day except we follow him as he leads us into the very depths of human need wherever we find it. As we follow him in faith, we shall surely hear the ancient admonition, "As you did it to one of the least of these my brethren, you did it to me."

We are summing up the revelation we find in the life of Christ when we say that a Christianity that leaves uncriticized and untouched the personal and social evils that cheapen, weaken, distort, and destroy men is a direct negation of this emphasis on a vital ethical faith. Those who honor the character of Christ can neither ignore nor take an indulgent attitude toward the use of alcohol, narcotics, and other drugs that weaken and finally destroy a wholesome personality. A vital faith will never ignore or treat indulgently anything that threatens marriage, the home, and the family. A vital faith will never stand idly by and let prejudices and bigotry tear the human family apart. It will be concerned honestly, openly, and deeply about the rights of every human being and every group of human beings in our society. This concern will articulate itself in terms of support for antipoverty programs, whether sponsored by government or philanthropic groups. The point is not who sponsors it, but who is to be benefited by it. This is always the point of Christian concern on matters like this. Even as the determined Christ set his face steadfastly toward Jerusalem and went there, despite the wails of fearful disciples, those who follow him today will find themselves led straight into the maelstrom of human need in our time. That is where we should be, for that is where he is.

V

If ever we are to have peace, if we are to participate effectively in the struggle for world community, we must make the proper beginning. We must begin where peace begins and always keep open our line of communication with it, for it is more than a point of departure; *it is our base of supplies.* This point of departure, this place where peace begins, is the kind of firm creative faith in God and man that we find in the character of our Lord.

Let us never forget that our only hope for peace begins with the renewal of belief in and loyalty to God as the author and guarantor of peace. Unless we honestly believe with all our heart, soul, mind, and strength that peace somehow represents God's will for mankind, we shall not long believe in the possibility of achieving it in a world like this. In fact, I am tempted to go so far as to say that the ultimate source of strength, steady enough to keep us at the endlessly difficult problems of world community is that of profound religious faith in the reality of God and his will for our peace. I do not mean that all men must share one set of religious beliefs in order to work together for peace. That obviously is not true. If it were, one has no notion whether peace would be possible at all. But I do mean that it makes all the difference in the world whether we believe that God has made peace possible, that he is working for it through us, and that he can turn even our mistakes on this matter to his own good purposes if we are willing to learn and to follow him.

If we believe that peace—the peace we seek—is not only made possible but actually guaranteed by the will of God for man, if we will search for him with all our hearts and are willing to find our way in his will, we will gain singleness of vision and purpose. Let us hope we may also gain that purity of heart of which Jesus speaks when he promises that those who are pure in heart shall see God. They become the peacemakers, the children of God!

# VI

"What does this mean in practical terms?" you ask. Several things come to mind in answer, the first of which is the recovery of integrity in our thought and efforts.

Integrity is the word to watch here. It is a little difficult to define, though I think it has a definite meaning to most of us when we see it. A number of years ago, Mr. George Nathan, famed Broadway critic, described a new play this way: "It has a fine integrity from beginning to end." By this he meant that it rang true, that there was a fundamental unity in thought, spirit, and development, that the entire play moved in an unforced manner toward the conclusion.

In like fashion, integrity means a tying together of life and work in a unity of purpose and action. When we are blessed with integrity—or to the degree that we are—we are delivered from the frustrating feeling that what we are building with our right hand we are tearing down with our left. We seek peace, pray for it, say we want it, yet actually nourish and prize the fears, hates, and desires that both make it impossible and, what is more, make it impossible for us to work for it effectively. We are, in Shakespeare's fine phrase, "double business bound" and are deeply and inwardly paralyzed by this fact. We are impaled in the spotlight of our miserable indecisions that are torn away by Elijah's blazing question, "How long will you go limping between two opinions?"

We begin to work for peace, then we learn sincerely to pray,

Create in me a clean heart, O God,
and put a new and right spirit within me.
(Psalm 51:10.)

Or as Francis of Assisi said, "Make me an instrument of thy peace, O God." If God should grant this petition and our relationship with him be kin to the petition, then our practical interests and actions would acquire a new center in peace and world community.

A thousand and one great problems, of course, would remain to be studied and solved if possible. But we would be able to face them with renewed confidence. We would be ready for them, not because we would have a blueprint of all necessary answers, but because we would have one thing only in mind as we approached the problems: peace and world community. All else would be subordinated to this. The lesser goals of race, nation, and way of life would be caught up and transformed in our determination to reach the greater goal.

Still another way to put the intensely practical value of faith in God as the author and guarantor of peace is this: It actually frees us inwardly to work for peace with all our energies. We can work for it as free men—freed from our fears, prejudices, half-gods, lesser loyalties, and thus be ready to be good instruments in the hands of God. No more limping along, crippled by indecision; no longer the unbearable division of life into faith on one hand against work on the other; but life

101

wholly, completely, unitedly trying to find its way in God's will. We cease being what William James once called "sick souls" in the presence of problems. Our doubts, fears, divisions, and hates disappear, and we become whole persons once more with energies of body, mind, and spirit gathered into a fine integrity for the tasks of working for world community.

All of this must sound hopelessly smug, self-righteous, and complacent, but the witness of all who have found themselves by first finding God is anything but that. Rather, they are humble, grateful, joyful workers. Eagerly expectant, they move into what to mortal eye is a dark and desperate future knowing that it is in God's hands and that he is trying to work out his will in it through people like them. Consequently, they are able to sing:

> God is my strong salvation;
> What foe have I to fear?

If ever we are to find peace and if ever we are to be instruments in the winning of world community, we must begin in humble adoration of him in whose will for peace we find both our peace and our will to work for peace without ceasing.

## VII

Coupled with the recovery of integrity through the rediscovery and renewal of our faith in God as the giver of peace comes the recovery of responsibility. This is important if we are to grapple with the vastness of the problem of achieving world community. Is it necessary to argue the reality of the need for a recovery of responsibility? Will not most of us admit that we have lost, or are rapidly losing, a keen sense of responsibility in this matter, not because we are lazy or unwilling to try to understand the problems we face, but because of the bewildering complexity of the problems themselves?

A number of years ago, Dr. Eugene Staley, a distinguished economist, put the matter very neatly in the course of a conversation he was having with some educators and clergymen. As I recall his remarks, he said, "If we could deal with the economics of peace by itself, we would come up with the answers in fairly short order. But the economics of peace fade into the politics of peace, and both fade into the deeper problems of ethics and the spirit of peace. Start in any of these areas and you find yourself immediately involved in all of them." Confronted by this fact, most of us, like the fabled Arabs, quietly fold our tents and silently steal away, hoping someone else will stay at the tasks that seem too complex for us. However, once we have recovered our sense of integrity by reuniting our will with God's purpose, we will discover that we are not able to betray the tasks at hand, for God is the one who sends us back to the job. In his sight and in the sight of those of us who love and serve him, there are no "faceless men" anywhere in the world. Anonymity is impossible. We are called by name and invited to give account of ourselves in person in the presence of the grave issues of our time. Those who seem to have known him best report that he does not expect us to play his role, but he does expect us to be human beings, his thoroughly responsible and obedient sons.

If responsibility is to mean anything at all in connection with the winning of world community, it requires that we be guided by the most realistic considerations possible. There is no reason why peace thought and action should wind up as they so frequently do—in the area of irrelevant idealism. The man who seeks peace should be the most realistic person on earth. Why should he be afraid of facts? Why should he not talk facts and nothing but facts when every important one is on his side?

To the skeptic who says peace is impossible, let us simply remind him that war is impossible if we are to survive. Peace is not only possible, but inevitable, if we are to survive. We are not talking now about the survival of the fittest, much less the survival of the righteous; we are talking about D-O-E-Day (death-of-earth-day) and facing the elemental fact that life cannot survive on this planet if we continue to go the way we are going.

The most important single force for peace now in existence is the United Nations, especially the many programs sponsored by the technical aid and assistance activities of that organization. When the critics of the U.N. have had their say and have made the most of the failures in the record of that organization, the towering fact remains that much good has been done and greater good remains to be done if nations continue to support the program. Of course, the program of the U.N. is costly—*it costs each one of us about ten cents a year!* Adding all of our dimes together, it has enabled us to spend many billions of dollars building roads, dams, spraying swamps, and vaccinating whole populations, as well as improving agricultural methods and performing many other useful services.

Let me quote again the most frequently quoted words in Pope Paul's address of October of 1965 to the United Nations: "No more war, war never again! Peace! It is peace which must guide the destinies of people and of all mankind." And, if you heard him, you could never forget the climax of what he said in his sermon at the Mass in Yankee Stadium: "We have three things to say to you. First of all, you must love peace. . . . Second, you must serve the cause of peace. . . . Third, peace must be based on moral and religious principles which will make it sincere and stable."

Let us then fall to the tasks at hand beginning by thanking God that *he is the God of peace* and praying with all our hearts, "Make me an instrument of thy peace." Having begun, in humble adoration at his throne, let us then band ourselves together in prayer, study, and work and stay together until in his mercy he has actually made us instruments of his peace. Then, let us, in all humility, be prepared to give him the honor and the glory.

## Chapter 6

# FIRMNESS

SCRIPTURE: Luke 11:17-23
TEXT: "He who is not with me is against me, and he who does not gather with me scatters."

## I

Occasionally we come across statements that seem to lay bare the very depths of our times. One such came recently from the pen of Dr. Margaret Mead, a distinguished anthropologist. She writes, "We are now at the point where we must educate people in what nobody knew yesterday and prepare in our schools for what no one knows yet, but what some people must know tomorrow."

This, surely, is both the impossible and inescapable character of the problem underlying the problems of our time. While we may need such wisdom, we know we will be a long time getting it. There are some things we need if we are ever going to gain this wisdom in the required amount—and firmness in our pursuit of it is one. This points directly to a quality in the character of Jesus Christ that leaps off every page of the four Gospels.

A recent novel by Taylor Caldwell refers to Luke as "Dear and Glorious Physician," and I suppose he does deserve that title. But we must not let it blind us to the fact that the Lord whom we meet in the Gospel of Luke is a master who firmly demands decision of all who meet him. Luke and his colleagues in writing the Gospels do not try to have their cake and eat it in this matter. The Christ they tell us about is an authentic master who confronts them with an invitation to discipleship in the building of the kingdom of God on earth. And he warns would-be disciples that in following him they are letting themselves in for a very rough time of it.

The firmness of Christ is seen in many ways in the Gospels, but never with greater clarity and force than in his decision to go to Jerusalem for what proved to be the last week of his life on earth.

No one made him go; in fact, everyone seems to have tried to dissuade him from the mad notion. His enemies warned and threatened him; his family and disciples pled with him; but he went. He set his face stead-fastly toward Jerusalem. Thomas cried, "Let us go also that we may die with him!" He went, and they followed.

He chose to go because he felt he could not complete his mission until he had stood in the Temple in Jerusalem during the Passover festival and proclaimed to his people that the kingdom of God was at hand. His firmness in doing this leaves no doubt that he felt it the call of God to do what he did. When God spoke to him, he listened and obeyed. He expected his disciples to do likewise.

He demanded a firm commitment of those who would follow him because he knew they lived in decisive days—days when the greatest thing that had ever happened in the history of mankind was taking place. God was inaugurating his kingdom! He was opening it to all who would meet the conditions of discipleship. His kingdom was at war with that of Satan and evil, and between them a man must choose.

We find and feel the firmness of our Lord wherever we encounter him in the Gospels. The New Testament is a record not only of what God is doing, but also of what he is trying to do in and through loyal souls. A sense of urgency broods over the early church—cosmic issues being joined in their very lives—an awareness that every man must choose for or against Christ.

We feel it especially in one incident related in Luke's

Gospel. The critics of our Lord were insinuating that his powers as healer and miracle worker might come from Satan rather than from God. In the thought of that day, Satan, too, had miraculous powers he could lend his representatives. That is why an ordinary man might be hard put to it to decide whether a miracle had been wrought by a good or an evil power.

Jesus answers, simply and clearly, that if he is a servant of Satan, he is betraying him because he is doing good—something Satan cannot do—and a house divided against itself cannot stand. Jesus concludes by demanding that his critics and other listeners stop asking idle questions and make up their minds where they stand. "He who is not with me is against me, and he who does not gather with me scatters" is his blunt way of summing up the matter.

Our Lord uses a metaphor drawn from the experience of a shepherd collecting a flock of sheep. A careful shepherd always collects his entire flock before he moves from pasture to fold, or from one pasture to another. If a thief desires to get his hands on some portion of the flock, he will make a loud noise to scatter them and then steal the ones he wants while the shepherd is trying to round up the rest.

Jesus is both issuing an invitation and conveying a solemn warning to his listeners. There is no neutral ground between God and Satan, between the kingdom of God and the kingdom of Satan. A neutral attitude toward Jesus and the kingdom of God is not possible.

You are either for or against him; you gather with him, or you scatter with his enemies. You simply cannot have it both ways—about this he is as firm as a rock. In it he rebukes not only those among his hearers who hated to make decisions but also those who thought that with a little judicious handling they might have it both ways—and thus avoid a costly decision.

Christians then and since have learned that firmness is a continuing quality in Christian life and character. We must make decisions for or against him all of the time. We are gathering with him or scattering with his enemies. His hand is firm, and if we would be Christians, we must make a firm commitment to him as Lord and Master.

Such convictions continue to be as costly as they were in the days when Luke and his comrades were trying to take the gospel throughout the Mediterranean world. They will richly repay a careful examination: first, in terms of what they meant then and, later, in terms of what they mean to us today.

II

It is the use of the word "Master" in the New Testament that should prepare us for the firmness we find in the relationship of Jesus Christ to his disciples and to everyone else. When Luke says that Jesus Christ is the actual Master of all who give him their loyalty, he is saying he is the potential Master of everyone else—beginning with all who will give him an honest hearing.

The word "Master" may not be the best word to apply to the loyalty which Jesus seeks of men. We have been reared in the disciplines of democracy, and we want none of the connotations of the master-slave, king-subject relationship. The late T. V. Smith, genial skeptic from the University of Chicago, once said that what religion needed was a democratic idea of God. In any event, the word "Master" creates shivers of apprehension in all who remember the recent ordeals with peoples obsessed with the idea that they were the "master" race.

In fact, the Revised Standard Version of the Bible usually drops the word "Master" in favor of "teacher," thus bypassing some objectionable connotations. But I am quite sure that Luke and the other writers of the Gospels would object to losing many of the meanings of Master from their presentation of Christ, for to Luke and all early Christians, he was the Master of men. When anyone asked these devoted folk, "Who is your Master?" they pointed unhesitatingly to Jesus Christ. Even when it meant the "fiery ordeals" spoken of in New Testament letters, or combats with wild beasts and gladiators in the Colosseum of Rome, the Christian answered, "He is our Master."

As we look at the idea of firmness in the Gospels, we will discover that it is a peculiar kind of relationship, and that explains why it is a continuing essential in Christian character. It exhibits certain characteristics of

Jesus Christ as Master and of the disciples as servants which sets their relationship worlds apart from ordinary relationships between leaders and followers.

To begin with, the firmness of Christ is based upon a compassionate understanding of people. One of the truest New Testament lines about him reads, "He knew what was in man." He was widely and intimately acquainted with people like us; that much is embarrassingly clear. We can find ourselves on almost any page of the Gospels. His knowledge of men was not a result of studying statistical tables about human behavior or reading books in biology. It came from a firsthand acquaintance with people. So far from trying to be impersonal in his approach to people, he was penetratingly personal. He approached them with understanding, concern, and affection. He reached out to them with an open hand, an open heart, and an open mind. Even spies and critics were given every chance to know him. He repelled no one because of the name he bore, the creed he professed, the race to which he belonged, or the cause he served.

This catholicity in approach and appeal to people made trouble for him and for his immediate disciples as it does for us today. The "righteous" people inveighed against him because he ate with "sinners." Peter and Paul fell into a violent disagreement over whether he was primarily the Savior of the Jews and, only secondarily, the Savior of the rest of the world. And, in our own time, we do not read far in church pronouncements before we discover that most churches insinuate that they have a special relationship to and claim on his beneficent influence in human life. But there is something about the magnitude of Jesus Christ that should put all such claims to shame. He is so much bigger than the men and institutions that have borne his name that we must all finally confess our inadequacy in the task of being his disciples.

Luke felt this powerful truth about Jesus' mastery of men in the preaching of Paul, as well as in the materials about the life and teachings of Jesus that lay before him as he wrote his Gospel. Consequently, he joined hands with Paul in the strong effort to free Jesus from the label of being simply the Jewish Messiah, or being especially concerned with some portion of the human race to the exclusion or subordination of the rest. Luke is both clear and firm on the point that while Jesus was the long-awaited Messiah of the Jews, he was infinitely more than that. He was, in truth, the Savior of the world. In him—Jew and Gentile, Greek, Roman, and barbarian, master and slave, men and women—all find the fulfillment of their spiritual quest.

> In Christ there is no East or West,
>   In him no South or North;
> But one great Fellowship of Love
>   Throughout the whole wide earth.

That is why the Christian church has presented Jesus Christ to the world as the master of all men and, from the beginning, has affirmed her faith in "one flock, one fold, one shepherd."

The mastery of Jesus is peculiar in still another sense. He does not seek to inflate his followers with conceit, pride, and self-righteousness as so frequently happens when the so-called masters of men address their devotees. Jesus sought to guide his followers into a firm understanding of the meaning of discipleship. Not for one moment did he coddle their sins and weaknesses. He held up for careful scrutiny the sins of good people, the evils committed in the name of virtue, and he did it with an effectiveness that has lost none of its force today. I know of no more relentless exposition of the sins of righteous people than that found in the parables of our Lord.

In the parables of the prodigal son, the good Samaritan, the Pharisee and the publican, Jesus did more than pronounce a judgment upon the sins of the evil scribes and Pharisees of his day. He posted a permanent warning for all who through the ages were to bear his name. The piercing insights of the parables make secular critics of the sins of religious people look like rank amateurs. Sinclair Lewis, for example, made quite a name for himself by pointing out the hypocrisies of religious people. He did so with a smirk and a sneer as he, too, passed by on the other side. One never feels that Lewis cared much about it, one way or another—a feeling wholly absent in Jesus Christ!

Because Jesus believed in God completely and sought to serve him faithfully and humbly with his entire life, he could feel the full tragedy of the elder brother in the parable of the prodigal son, or of the ones who passed by on the other side in the parable of the good Samaritan, or of the Pharisee in the parable of the two men who went up to the Temple to pray. He did not merely "note" these evils. He brought down the judgment of Almighty God upon them and warned his hearers against them—and these warnings still stand.

Jesus Christ demanded sincerity as well as loyalty of those who stepped to his side. He asked them to do an about-face in this business of living and do it with conviction and joy. He sought no verbal disciples—men who would say the right things and then let the matter drop. He must have been impressed with the large number of his contemporaries who felt free to say, "Lord, Lord," yet do little or nothing about it. He demanded that men do something about their faith in God. When the lawyer, whose question had led to the parable of the good Samaritan, confessed that the one who had helped the man in need was his neighbor, Jesus said, "Go and do likewise." When a well-favored ruler came to him, plagued by the saving awareness of something lacking in his life, Jesus pointed out the trouble. Something had come between him and God, and he had to get rid of it. In this case, it was his pos-

116

sessions. Jesus said, "Go, sell what you have, and give to the poor, and you will have treasure in heaven." To would-be disciples who were holding back, some for one reason, some for another, he issued the discerning but blunt warning, "No one who puts his hand to the plow and looks back is fit for the kingdom of God."

Jesus exerted a firm mastery over the whole range of life because he never let anyone think he was doing the work of the kingdom of God when he was merely repeating words about it. Some disciples have been tempted to forget that there is an enormous difference between the train announcer who calls out the destinations of the trains that are leaving the station and the people who actually get on the trains to make the trip.

Still another characteristic of his mastery is found in the New Testament. We must *volunteer* to follow him, for his is an open and free fellowship of faith, understanding, and life. We cannot force that kind of loyalty and fellowship. It is a gift—a gift based upon conviction, understanding, and joy. Much as Jesus might have loved the well-favored ruler who sought eternal life, much as he might have desired him to be among his disciples, much as he was disappointed when "he went away sorrowful," Jesus confronted him with the choice he alone could make if he would be a disciple—and he made no effort to soften the choice in order to be sure the man stayed with him. Obviously, Jesus would not, if he could have done so, force the decision on this man, but he could and did clarify the issue that had to be faced.

So far as I can understand the Gospel records, our Lord never tried to lure anyone into the company of the disciples by saying, in effect, "Come on in. You might just as well be with us as not. Not too much will be expected of you if you join." Jesus could never have reasoned that way because he intended that discipleship should make all the difference in the world. Nor did he tell would-be disciples they should come in because it was "the thing to do," that it would help them socially, financially, or professionally, when he knew that membership in that fellowship was certain to be accounted the shame and disgrace Peter discovered it to be as he sought to warm his hands at a fire in the courtyard of the Temple the night before the Crucifixion.

Jesus put the matter of discipleship squarely, openly, and honestly: "If any man would come after me, let him deny himself and take up his cross daily and follow me. For whoever would save his life will lose it; and whoever loses his life for my sake, he will save it." He required of all would-be disciples a clean-cut decision. To those who wanted to have it both ways, who were inclined to compromise or straddle on the matter of complete loyalty, he said, "No one can serve two masters; for either he will hate the one and love the other, or he will be devoted to the one and despise the other. You cannot serve God and mammon."

## III

It is not too difficult, is it, to see why men, then and now, are reluctant to follow such a master? His intention is clear: the establishment of a new relationship between man and God; the transformation of the world through that relationship, beginning with and working through people like us; the creation of a body of disciples who will work at this task until it was done. Rather, they will be the ones through whom God could work until his kingdom has come on earth. And Jesus was firm about it!

Does history record anywhere a more incredible scene than that in which Jesus takes leave of his disciples? As Luke reconstructs it in the opening chapter of the book of Acts, eleven men gathered around him on Mount Olivet outside Jerusalem to hear him say, "You shall be my witnesses in Jerusalem and in all Judea and Samaria and to the end of the earth." Look at that handful of men (poor, unlearned peasants and artisans, weaponless, few in number) and reflect on his words, "to the end of the earth," and tell me, you realists: What would you give for their chances of fulfilling his high hopes for them? Not much, would you? But they did just that!

We are shoddy heirs if we are content to rejoice in what they did when lying squarely on our doorstep today is the unfinished work which they have so nobly carried on. We will not want to volunteer for the role of

Christian discipleship in a casual moment or mood. We know what it means: It is a freely chosen relationship of loyalty and joy; it is centered in Jesus Christ; it is a commitment of one's life to the building of the kingdom of God. This is a way of saying that Christian discipleship, when taken seriously, requires a rethinking of life and society and a recentering of both life and society in the will of God as we see it in Jesus Christ. This, easily, is the most radical proposal ever made to man. Lay it alongside the so-called radical proposals of thinkers like Marx and Lenin, and they seem conservative by comparison!

We shall not want to delude ourselves for one moment in thinking that the world is waiting with open arms for the work of Christian disciples. We are living in a fool's paradise if we think individuals, institutions, and nations will welcome the firm purpose of the Christian church to proclaim the gospel without fear or favor wherever men are. It is as much of a fight now as it was in the first century to get a hearing for the Christian gospel. We who work in the Christian church must face that fact as we go about the ancient task of trying to find our way in the will of God as we see it in Jesus Christ. Men continue to fear, resent, and hate the judgments which must be passed upon them from this perspective. They continue to react violently toward Christians, Christian attitudes, Christian positions, and Christian institutions which press this judgment.

It will not come as news to you that there are many in the membership of Christian churches today who shrink from the encounters now being forced upon the church by firm loyalty to the ideals and the leadership of Jesus Christ. They want the church to be a pallid reflection of hallowed prejudices and beloved ways of life. We do not mind hearing other people and other ways of life brought under the stinging judgments of Christian criticism, but spare our own! Consequently, the serenity of Christian fellowship is badly disturbed over the race question, the question of subversion within the churches, and the problem of how much initiative the church should take in keeping men conscious of the great issues of our time.

It was only fifteen years ago when a group of influential and dedicated laymen attached to the National Council of Churches sought to secure from the General Board of that body the assurance that neither the General Board nor any of its committees nor any group called into being by the National Council would make public any recommendations regarding social, political, economic, or international issues. When the General Board rejected this ultimatum almost without a dissenting vote, the ones who sent it withdrew from the National Council, and many of them withdrew from their churches.

There is no escaping this kind of unpleasantness and division in the life of the church so long as there

121

are those who would have the church shrink away from involvement in the issues that are breaking the minds and the spirits of men. Clearly, the church cannot and will not do it. While she prizes unbroken fellowship as one of her great goals, there is a greater one—namely, firm loyalty to and obedience to Jesus Christ.

Why, we ask ourselves, do churches get involved in such dark, difficult, and divisive issues? One answer must be made—and it is adequate: Because God is involved in them! And he expects those who name his name to get in and stay involved until the kingdom of love has found some kind of effective expression in and through us. I wish there were another way—an easier way—but I know of none. Of one thing I am sure as a Christian minister: I will never concern myself with problems that do not concern people. Nor can I avoid the other side of the coin: I will always concern myself as intelligently and as forcefully as I know how with every problem that does relate to the children of God anywhere on the face of this earth.

## IV

However, we misunderstand the genius of the Christian faith and the character it seeks to nurture if we think of it primarily as an indictment of evil. Basically, it is the proclamation of the good news of the kingdom of God, a kingdom of love, in which we are invited to enter as full citizens and communicants. It does not exhaust itself in denouncing evil; it concentrates the main thrusts of its efforts and attention upon overcoming evil with good—first, in our own lives and then in the life of society. This, of course, is the hardest part of the discipline of Christian discipleship, and it is the kind of task that never stays done. We will work at it all of the time and so will our children. Yet, from the beginning, acceptance of the discipline of firm loyalty to Jesus Christ has been the distinctive thing about Christian character and the Christian church. The Stoics of Greece and Rome beheld the evils in their beloved cities and country and cried, "Look what the world is coming to!" The early Christians looked out upon the same scene, lifted Jesus Christ high, and cried, "Look what is coming to the world!"

What was coming? One who knew God; one who was the way, the truth, and the life; one who meant more to his disciples than all of the rest of the world; one who was the Master of men and who deserved to be followed because he pointed the way to God and his kingdom.

And how was he coming? In clouds of glory? Armed by angelic hosts? No. He was being brought in and through the love, the devotion, and the loyalty of a company of people who hailed him as Master. If he is to be brought to our day, it will be by a similar company—and there is a place in it for each person. The question we face is quite simple: Are we ready to make a firm decision to find and fill our place in the fellowship of those who believe that in Jesus Christ we have the life, the truth, and the way to the will of God for all mankind?

## Chapter 7
# TRIUMPH*

SCRIPTURE: Matthew 28:1-18

## I

On this glad morn we greet each other with the ancient shout of triumph, "Hallelujah, Christ is risen!" The greatness of the victory Christians celebrate today is beyond dispute. It has stood the hardest of all tests—the test of time. For nearly twenty centuries an increasing number of people all over the world have hailed it the most meaningful victory known to man. Today, nearly nine hundred million people lift up their souls, crying in every language known to man, "Hallelujah! Christ is risen!" Even in countries where atheism is the official philosophy of the government, the churches

---

\* An Easter sermon.

will be crowded with people saying the prayers we say, singing the songs we sing, thanking God, even as we do, for Jesus Christ and his triumph over sin and death. In England, where less than ten percent and here in America where barely fifty percent of the people are actively interested in churches, a vastly greater percentage will find their way to sunrise services and services of worship in churches to join in the celebration of the greatest victory known to man. In truth, it is "deep calling unto deep"—the deepest and truest thing God ever said calling insistently to men like us with the deepest and truest word we have ever heard regarding the nature and meaning of our life. Other great men and moments have come; they have known their hour of blazing glory, then grown dim with time—but not so with the triumph of Easter. Starting as a pinpoint of light in the vast darkness of human life, it has grown steadily until today, truly, it is the light of the world.

Yet, an honest celebration of this victory requires us to leave the realm of superlatives and come down to this workaday world where it actually happened. We must, if we can and as far as we are able, try to understand why it has always meant so much to us.

If we will study with some care the character of Jesus Christ as it defined itself in life, we will discover not one, but a succession of very human and almost commonplace triumphs which came, as it were, to glorious climax on Easter morning. I say "human and almost commonplace" because we, too, as we seek to be his dis-

126

ciples, must engage in the same battles and win, if we can, the same victories. It is possible to understand the claim he made to his disciples: "Be of good cheer, I have overcome the world," for he had done just that! Whenever we think of him, the word "triumph" comes to mind. For despite the fact he died on the cross and was deserted by his followers at the time, we cannot think of him without sensing the overtones of victory and triumph in who he was and what he did.

## II

"What victories did he win?" we ask, and the Gospels give answer.

To begin with, he was victorious over the temptation to avoid the cross. He must have known from the very beginning of his public ministry that he was headed for trouble. His family and followers knew it, and his enemies spelled it out with increasing clarity from time to time, beginning with the very first sermon he ever preached. It could not have been easy to persist in the face of all this. Yet, he did! He was victorious over the temptation to stay in Galilee; to enjoy the peace and quiet of the carpenter shop and the comforts of home; to ply his own trade; to mind his own business; to save his own skin—if we want to put it that way. He was either unacquainted with or unimpressed by what someone has called the "eleventh commandment" today, namely, "Don't stick out your neck!" He did, and he was aware of what he was doing. Despite the entreaties of family and friends, he set his face steadfastly toward Jerusalem for the final, unavoidable encounter between his strenuous spiritual idealism and the religious and political powers there entrenched.

He was not taken to Jerusalem under arrest. He went of his own will and choice. If ever a man moved into a trap, he did. When he entered the storied gates of the city, the chains snapped shut in a matter of hours after Roman and Jewish authorities knew of his presence there. Put ourselves in his place or if we cannot bring ourselves to that even in imagination, let us join his followers on that journey from the security of Nazareth to the dangers of Jerusalem, from the warm bosom of family to the loud controversy of mobs, from the loyalty of a few friends to the hot anger of many enemies, from the pleasantness of life to the bitterness of death. As we walk in that company, we will understand—at least from afar—the costliness of his triumph over the temptation to stay in Galilee.

Once he was in Jerusalem, the fight went on, and it had to be won in still another way. He had to triumph over the temptation to quit at the last minute. Who could have blamed him if he had done just that? None of us, surely. Look at what was going on! His disciples were confused and wavering. One had already deserted and betrayed him; he had no reason to think that the rest would stay as the crisis worsened. His enemies were sure of their ground; they had an airtight case against him and the power to do whatever they wanted to do.

As that last week wore on, Jesus was obsessed with the feeling of being alone, of being "one against the world" —so much so that his sense of loyalty was shaken. The temptation to quit at the last minute reached its climax in the Garden of Gethsemane. How easy it would have been for him to slip out of that Garden on the eastward road even as the soldiers were coming up from the west! Standing, rather, kneeling, there between two roads and two worlds and all that they meant, he prayed, "Father, if thou art willing, remove this cup from me; nevertheless not my will, but thine, be done." I am overwhelmed by the costliness of this struggle each time I read Luke's simple words, "And being in an agony he prayed more earnestly; and his sweat became like great drops of blood falling down upon the ground." But he won!

Even then his struggle was not over. He had to resist the temptation to curry Pilate's favor. He must have known that his only chance to get Pilate to set him free was to say the right thing—to do a bit of public crawling! Pilate hated religious quarrels. He would have none of them in his court if he could avoid them. He demanded loyalty to Caesar, and when that was guaranteed, he was through.

If Jesus had been willing to make one or two conciliatory statements, there is every reason to think that he would have been released. He might have said,

"Pilate, I swear I have no quarrel with Rome. Let Rome rule the bodies of men; I am interested only in their souls." Or, he might have said, "The trouble here is purely religious; it deals with nothing that concerns Rome." Or, "Why, I am loyal to Caesar! I say, 'Render unto Caesar the things that are Caesar's and unto God the things that are of God!' There's no conflict in loyalty between the two."

When I consider the frequency with which Christians have said things like these over the centuries, quoting him as authority, I marvel at the fact that he never said them himself upon this occasion when they would have made the difference between life and death. But he could not say them because he knew that when one is truly concerned about the souls of men, one cannot and will not ignore their bodies and their bodily needs. He knew—and we are finding it out—that a conflict in loyalties is inevitable whenever Caesar demands absolute loyalty. That should be given to God alone. No state has a right to ask it, and when one does, it must be defied.

With his life at stake, Jesus was victorious over the temptation to try to escape the cross by means of such dodges, evasions, and half-truths. He earned the right to say, "I have overcome the world."

## III

Arrested, tried, sentenced, and on his way to the cross—surely that should have ended his temptations.

It did mark the end of some, but not all. Actually, there still lay before him the struggle over two temptations that rout us completely when we meet them—as meet them we must in his service.

He was victorious over the temptation to hate those who hated him. His fellow prisoners might rail and curse at their captors, but there is no record that he even so much as thought of doing so. When I consider how normal the instinct to retaliate in kind is, I wonder all the more at his prayer, "Father, forgive them; for they know not what they do." There is no trace of vengeance or animosity in it; it is the fulfillment of his conviction that we should love our enemies, bless those who curse us, and pray for those who despitefully use us. By so doing, Jesus set before his followers one of the loftiest ethical standards known—the forgiveness of, and prayers for, one's enemies; a life devoid of enmity, hatred, and malice. His disciples, then and now, have never fully accepted this standard, but we have caught enough of its spirit never to be able to hate and seek revenge without knowing that there is something tragically wrong in what we are doing.

Despite the fact that his disciples were scattered, his death now certain, his dreams of the kingdom coming in power in his lifetime apparently at an end, Jesus was victorious over the temptation to lose faith in man and God. He looked beneath the surface of his followers' vacillations and detected their firm conviction and strong will; he was confident that he could build on that faith, as on a strong rock, and that the gates of hell would not prevail against it. He was certain they would carry on, and they did.

He accepted the old, old fact that God moves in his own way and, sometimes, his way is past our finding out—at least ahead of the event itself. As a final act in Jesus' earthly life, he found his peace in the will of God, saying, "Into thy hands, I commit my spirit."

Since that time the final posture of Christian character in the face of defeat and death has been one of trust and confidence in the power of God. Confidence in the triumph of the will of God is worlds removed from a spirit of resignation or fatalism. It is the simple affirmative faith that the God of the universe will use whatever of worth there is in whatever of worth we are and whatever of merit there is in what we try to do. This faith is no substitute for action; rather it is both the invitation to and the climax of action. Jesus had lived in God; he was dying in God. He was content and at peace with himself, his fellowmen, and his God.

## IV

Then came Easter morning with the great good news that God had wrestled victory out of defeat—life out of death. Small wonder the fragmentary records we have of this event do not tell a smoothly connected story, complete in every detail. The details differ all along the line, but there is real unity in the meaning that the

Gospels are trying to express—that in this incredible triumph the entire outlook for the human race was changed, changed because he had triumphed over the two great enemies of all men: sin and death.

"He broke the power of sin!" the early Christians cried to a generation that was searching feverishly for deliverance from sin. Name the sins that corrupt life— greed, lust, hate, fear—he breaks the power of them all. How? By leading us into the proper relationship with God, by encouraging us to believe that we actually can live with God, and by demanding a decision for or against God's will. Knowing how firm a hold sin has on life, Jesus promises no easy conquest of it, but he gives us confidence that it can be done.

Dr. Claude Montifiore, a distinguished Jewish scholar, singled out Jesus' concern for the sinner as the distinctive thing about him. "Jesus not only loved the sinner; he actually sought him out, bringing him new confidence in himself and in his power to master his sins." That, I am sure, is why the gospel has been called the "gospel of the second chance." Only it might well be called the "gospel of yet another chance" because it holds that anyone, no matter what he has been or what he has done, can make a fresh start at this business of living. No man's case is ever hopeless before God. No man is permitted the luxury of saying, "There is nothing I can do to change what I am." In other words, we do not have the right either to quit in despair because of what we are or to be satisfied with what we are and what we are doing. Jesus makes it plain that God never gives up trying to open the doors to a new life for all men. He sets before all "an open door," and no one can close it—not even man himself.

It is the testimony of men for over two thousand years that the triumph we celebrate on this glad Easter Day is a victory over the power of sin in human life. As a result of it, men like Paul, Augustine, William Booth, John Wesley, and a host of others have cast off the shackles of sin and walked as free men—made free by Jesus Christ. And to us who today feel the selfsame shackles, the promise still holds: "Find your way in the love of God as seen in Jesus Christ, and you will know the meaning of spiritual freedom. Greed, lust, hate, fear—these destroyers and their power can be broken in your life. Truth can conquer falsehood; peace can triumph over war; love can triumph over hate."

If we doubt whether it is possible for us to share in this great victory that overcomes the world, then hear this testimony of one of our contemporaries.

Power—the power to create a new world resides in Jesus of Nazareth—and countless men and women since have found power for their special service in him. Spiritual regeneration means, above all else, the communication of that life and power to the souls of men. How this takes place may be a mystery. Men may explain it in different terms, and sometimes they seem almost contradictory to each other. But they agree in confessing that such illumination and power as have come to them has, in some way, come as they have been drawn near to and assimilated something of the spirit of Jesus Christ, the Savior of the world. . . . It is he who has been acknowledged as guide and leader, as the strength in every hour of need, and as the source of all that is best and truest. It is he to whom every race and kindred have come in acknowledgment that he is Lord and Savior.

Truly, he has "overcome the world."

## V

The triumph of Jesus Christ was not in some never-never world, but in this world. It was not over some imaginary sins, but over the ones that set us over against each other in mortal hate and strife. The sins he met head on were and are prejudice, sectarian strife, hatred of man for man, and the spirit of vengeance.

These are sins and must be overcome if God's new world is ever to come the only way it can come—through the love, devotion, and loyalty of persons like us. It is the faith of Easter that Jesus Christ overcame sins like these and did so in a completely realistic sense, for he met them squarely, exposed them as evil, refused to be governed by them, and bade his followers to be vigilant in their struggle against them.

His triumph is seen in this: The struggle to keep

faith with him and to be obedient to his leading is a vital part of the life of each one of us and of every Christian church. He has won the victory over the sin of separatism in Christendom; in fact, he is that victory. As the several hundred Christian churches approach each other now, it is with a sense of acute shame over our separateness and a consciousness of our unity in him. We know that he has triumphed over our sectarian rivalries, and we are trying to find out how to spell this victory out in terms of our actual church life and relationships, for when we come to him, we come together or not at all. I cannot believe for a single moment that he is interested in Christians more than in Jews or in Protestants more than in Catholics. And there is not a shred of evidence to indicate that he might be. He won a victory for the spirit of man in all men and for faith in God in all the religions of the world.

In his name, then, let us get on with the job of losing our life for his sake in this world as it is, so that the world of which he taught and for which he lived and died may live again in vision and in fact. He can and will win the victory over poverty, want, illness, prejudice, hate, violence, and war, and we are the ones in and through whom this victory is being spelled out today. We are not neglecting our faith as we work at these evils within and among us; we are honoring and obeying him.

It comes down to these daily disciplines: As we

work at our realistic problems of illness and the disciplines of health, the great Physician, whether known or unknown, acknowledged or unacknowledged, is our guide and guard.

As we address ourselves to the problems that separate us from each other in creed, nation, race, and ideology, we are not forgetting him; we are remembering him. We are not ignoring him; we are acknowledging him.

As pope, prelate, priest, minister, and rabbi come together to plead for peace and to discover the road toward the time when men "will war no more, and none shall make them afraid," we are proclaiming God's victory over the very sins that men once took for granted, even accepted fatalistically as a part of life. In Jesus Christ we have discovered the evil, the sinful nature of everything that makes for war—and, in his name, we now declare unremitting, unrelenting war on war, pledging never to lay down our weapons of love and conciliation until "every foe is vanquished, and Christ is Lord indeed."

Easter is not something that happened solely at another time, in another place, in another age; it is happening here and now, in persons like us. Because of him

> We've a story to tell to the nations
> That shall turn their hearts to the right,
> A story of truth and mercy,
> A story of peace and light.

We've a message to give to the nations
That the Lord who reigneth above
Hath sent his Son to save us
And show us that God is love.

And this is the faith in which we work and in which we will win:

For the darkness shall turn to dawning
And the dawning to noonday bright,
And Christ's great kingdom shall come on earth,
The kingdom of love and light.

## VI

We celebrate his triumph over the fear of death—sometimes called the "last enemy." Let us, in all humility, try to clarify the nature of this victory. Death remains. To be born is to die; to live is to die. To love is to know the meaning of grief and loneliness when death takes our beloved. All this is unchanged, and no power on earth or elsewhere can change it. But the fear of it all, the sense of despair over it, the feeling that death ends all and brings life to a full stop, that it puts an ultimate end to dear and treasured relationships—all of this has been changed by the conquest of the fear of death through Jesus Christ.

Yet, I would not leave the impression that the pall of death has been lifted by some kind of magical transaction on the cross. In his life and teachings Jesus approached the problem of death with sympathetic and penetrating spirit. We have never been able to think of death as the "grim reaper" since he taught us to regard it as a door which opens on life eternal. Where is there room for fear of death if it is like a friendly inn—an eternal home with room for all? When we are tempted to fear death, let us remember his words of assurance to troubled disciples as he and they faced openly the fact of his approaching death: "Let not your hearts be troubled; believe in God, believe also in me. In my Father's house are many rooms [The Greek actually reads, "There are rooms enough for all"]; . . . I go to prepare a place for you. . . . I will come again and take you where I am."

Where is there room for fear of death in this approach to the end of life? This is the spirit that overcomes the fear of death! Who can fear death—for himself or for his loved ones—after hearing it described as a traveler coming home at the end of the day and greeted with the words, "Well done, good and faithful servant, enter thou into thy rest." Dying is going home at evening time, where loved ones and old friends, whom we have loved and lost awhile, are gathering, where the real issues of life and death are resolved, where the peace of God reigns.

Robert Louis Stevenson penned a profoundly Christian line when he wrote, "When one believes in God, where is any room for fear?" Certainly there is no room for fear in a faith like that of Bishop William Lawrence, written shortly before his death:

I know that my Heavenly Father is love, justice, and truth. I believe that Jesus Christ lived that I might learn of Him, follow Him, and pass through the gates of death with Him and in His eternal company. With this clear and final confidence, what have I to fear from man, misfortune, disease, and sorrow? In perfect faith one may live on toward the setting of the sun—tranquil and in perfect serenity.

Or hear this prayer of a young man, a devout Christian, who had just learned that his days were to be cut short by a fatal disease,

O giver of life on earth and in Heaven, thou who hast breathed of thine own spirit, my call to go has come, and I am on the edge of a lonely margin . . . . Fortify me to meet death as I ought; as Christ would have me. . . . O Father, enfold in thy loving, everlasting arms my beloved and gallant wife, boy, and precious little daughters. I know thou wilt. . . . Thy love is deeper than the deepest sea, and it has no ebb or flow. . . . Receive me as into thy hands I entrust myself, and to thy name be glory and praise, through Jesus Christ, my Savior.

Let the artists tell us what they find in the Christian conception of death. One of our own poets, Robert Nathan, has done this in a hauntingly beautiful poem,

"Last Game," based upon the game of hide-and-seek which we played when we were children.

Fauré does the same thing in his own medium. His *Requiem* put to music the Christian interpretation of death. It begins by plumbing the depths of sorrow, separation, and tragedy, which always seem to swallow up life. Slowly and surely the mood and the music move upward from doubt through faith, from questioning toward trust, until finally it bursts into the warmth and loveliness of a tender lullaby. It begins with a sense of tragedy and agony; it ends with a sense of peace and contentment. From beginning to end it breathes the confidence of our Lord: "I have overcome the world."

He continues to invite his disciples to share in this wondrous victory. If we want to accept, we must be prepared to lose our life for the sake of the gospel; to die with him in order to rise with him—it is as ancient, as simple, as revolutionary, and as contemporary as that!

I take it to be more than a left-handed compliment to Jesus Christ that many of those in our time who seem willing and able to give up God still cling to Jesus Christ. This, as I understand it, is a way of acknowledging that if he goes, all goes; that in some deep and dimly sensed way he is our truest insight into the deepest meanings of life. As long as he is, we are—and can hope to become other and better than we are.

So today we celebrate the triumph of Jesus Christ.

141

Some will say in childlike faith, "Christ is risen"; and others will say, "As long as I can believe in him and walk with him, I can believe in myself and in you, and we can learn how to walk together and with him into the unknown and ominous future." As I believe in the God whom I find in Jesus Christ, both statements of faith are acceptable in his sight.

Let us, then, share in the triumphant victory which was wrought out in the sin-redeeming, death-conquering life, death, and resurrection of Jesus Christ. It is the victory of truth over falsehood, hope over fear, love over hate, and life over death. Far from being "mere abstractions," as some may think, these are the only victories that are really concrete. Far from being negligible, as some may think, they are the only victories that really count. They are universal; they can and must be won in the life of every person. They are victories over the perpetual evils which seek to stifle and distort life in all men, over those very evils which, even now, cause us to hurl ourselves at each other in the fury of suspicion, hate, and conflict.

One of the strangest things about this triumph can be put this way: It proceeds, not by the taking of life, but by the giving and the enriching of life. In all other kinds of victory known to man, let us be prepared to repent in sackcloth and ashes. But in this victory alone let us rejoice and thank God for him who earned the right to say, "Be of good cheer, I have overcome the

142

world." From the first Easter the accent has been on life, the good life, life eternal—and there it must and will remain for all who believe in Jesus Christ and who stand up this day to cry out, "Hallelujah! Christ is risen!"